SPAS & HOT TUBS, SAUNAS & HOME GYMS

SPAS & HOT TUBS, SAUNAS & HOME GYMS

Tom Cowan
Jack Maguire

CREATIVE HOMEOWNER PRESS®

Current printing (last digit)
10   9   8   7   6   5   4   3   2

Produced by Roundtable Press, Inc.

Directors: Marsha Melnick, Susan E. Meyer
Editorial: Don Nelson, Marguerite Ross
Design: Jeffrey Fitschen
Photo Research: Martha Richheimer
Cover Design: Jerry Demoney
Front Cover Photo: Jerry Demoney for Stockpile, Inc.
Front Cover Photo Stylist: Ann Demoney for Stockpile, Inc.
Illustrations: Norman Nuding
Art Production: Nadina Simon

LC: 88-20216
ISBN: 0-932944-85-X (paper)
          0-932944-87-6 (hardcover)

CREATIVE HOMEOWNER PRESS®
BOOK SERIES
A DIVISION OF FEDERAL
MARKETING CORPORATION
24 PARK WAY,
UPPER SADDLE RIVER, NJ 07458

Acknowledgments

The editors of Creative Homeowner Press would like to thank the following individuals, contributors, and companies who have assisted in the preparation of this publication:

Almost Heaven™ Hot Tubs, Ltd.
Route 250
Renick, WV 24966

Arizona Custom Pools & Landscaping
1528 East Missouri
Suite 101
Phoenix, AZ 85014

B & B Pool and Spa Center
787 Chestnut Ridge Road
Chestnut Ridge, NY 10977

Barrel Builders
1085 Lodi Lane
St. Helena, CA 94574

California Pools & Spas
4600 North Santa Anita Avenue
El Monte, CA 91731

Classic Pool & Patio
5294 East 65th Street
Indianapolis, IN 46220

Cording Landscape Design, Inc.
226 Franklin Turnpike
Ramsey, NJ 07446
Len DiTomaso, ASLA

Creative Energy
11 Commercial Boulevard
Novato, CA 94947

Creative Environments, Inc.
PO Box 586
Alamo, CA 94507

Ann Demoney
Jerry Demoney
Stockpile, Inc.
52 Maltbie Avenue
Suffern, NY 10901

Susan Dufford
Creative Homeowner Press

Dolphin Pool Supply & Service
3544 Forest Lane
Dallas, TX 75234

Phillip H. Ennis Photography
2935 Dahlia Avenue
Baldwin Harbor, NY 11510

Carol Hart
Schlott Realtors
Saddle River, NJ

Hot Tubs International
8486-H Tyco Road
Vienna, VA 22180

Mr. and Mrs. Joseph Laurite

Mission Valley Pools & Spas, Inc.
6121 Mission Gorge Road
San Diego, CA 92120

National Spa & Pool Institute
2111 Eisenhower Avenue
Alexandria, VA 22314

Barbara Ostrom, ASID
Upper Saddle River, NJ

Perma-Built
627 Route 23
Pompton Plains, NJ 07444
Charlotte Dietrich

Dr. and Mrs. Kalman Post

Sauna Factory
Sterling Mine Road
Sloatsburg, NY 10974

The Spa Shop
213 Route 206 North
Flanders, NJ 07836
Karl Schoenwalder

Spas by Renée
2625 East Tropicana Avenue
Las Vegas, NV 89121

Jessie Walker Photography
241 Fairview Road
Glencoe, IL 60022

Introduction

Millions of Americans are committed to physical well-being as an essential part of life. For many this means regular workouts with exercise equipment. For others it includes relaxation in a spa or hot tub after a hard day's work or other exertion. And for a growing number the stimulation and rejuvenation of a sauna bath crown the day's routines.

This book shows you how you can incorporate spas, hot tubs, saunas, and exercise rooms, and the good health and happiness that go with them, into your home. The projects described here show you how to create the environments in which you and your family can exercise, relax, unwind, or entertain. The step-by-step instructions give you a sense of the time, money, space, and skills needed to fulfill your needs. There are also plenty of suggestions to stimulate your imagination in adapting general principles to personal preferences.

Chapter 1 of this book introduces you to the exciting world of hydrotherapy: the spa and the hot tub. Both are tubs designed for leisure soaking in hot, aerated water. Both can be installed indoors or out, above or below ground level. The projects in this chapter show step-by-step procedures for installing a hot tub and a spa. The hot tub project explains how to assemble a regular hot tub purchased from one of the many hot tub companies that will send you all the parts in ready-to-assemble kits.

The spa project shows how to sink a fiberglass spa into the ground so that the top is flush with a patio. Also explained are the components of the support system and the advantages and disadvantages of skid packs versus individually bought and assembled pieces.

In Chapter 2, the basics of sauna construction are outlined for homeowners who wish to build one using

either their own materials or a complete prefab kit from one of the many sauna suppliers in the U.S.

The secret of a successful sauna depends on two things: a well-sealed room that retains heat and a stove powerful enough to generate the heat needed for the size of the room. The most popular stoves for home saunas are the electric stoves, but gas stoves and traditional wood-burning stoves with their mystique and romance are still suitable for certain settings. The pros and cons of each are fully explained.

In addition to an indoor sauna project (building a sauna yourself in the basement), the chapter includes instructions for pouring footings, framing walls and roofs, and building a shower stall should you choose to build a sauna hut outside. What to look for in a prefab sauna kit and instructions on how to take a sauna round out the chapter.

Chapter 3 deals with the fitness center par excellence: the home exercise room. It discusses exercise areas that are independent rooms as well as those that are part of another room. It also presents the various exercise equipment available on the market and explains how to shop for value. It suggests the basic equipment needed for a total body program, showing how,

with a minimum of equipment, it is possible to develop a fitness program to keep in shape.

Guidelines are offered for designing and decorating the room where you will keep and use your exercise devices. A handy grid, together with cut-out templates of various pieces of furniture and equipment, lets you arrange individual items on a floor plan so you can determine what designing you'll need to do.

Chapter 4 is a manual for water and equipment care. It discusses the rudiments of water maintenance, detailing how to balance water chemically and use the proper disinfectants to keep it sanitized. It suggests daily, weekly, and monthly programs for maintaining clean, healthy water. You will learn about pH, alkalinity, and water hardness, and how to use and store chemicals safely.

Chapter 4 also outlines the basic care required to clean hot tubs and spas and keep them in peak operating condition. It explains how to make simple repairs for both tubs and spas.

Most of the projects described in this book constitute major home improvements and property alterations. When done properly, they can become home fitness and relaxation centers that will provide you and your family with years of enjoyment.

CONTENTS

The spacious, semicircular deck and benches surrounding this hot tub offer a splendid vantage point from which to view the wide open vista beyond.

A brightly-tiled spa, benches, and lattice wall are unified on a compact octagon that occupies one end of this broad, elevated deck.

A circular spa and an adjacent free-form pool set a few feet below occupy nearly all of this backyard, which is snugly enclosed by shrubs and trees.

This hot tub sits in a cozy back corner of a house surrounded by attractive decking, brick, and wood siding.

Massive concrete blocks covered by glistening, glazed tile support this large spa; a tangle of flowering shrubs offers a colorful textural contrast.

Rugged boulders and flowering plants break up the severe lines of tile and cement that surround this five-sided spa and fountain.

Warm wood and plush carpeting create a luxurious setting for this indoor spa; the changing outdoor scene floods in through generous windows.

Vast expanses of glass, accented on all sides by lush potted plants, turn this large spa into a sunny greenhouse.

The wood decking of this patio invites bathers to a small spa after a swim in the nearby pool.

A simple hot tub fills the corner of this sunny indoor relaxation room.

This paneled exercise room combines the latest in equipment with a spa and an old-fashioned woodburning stove to ease winter's chill.

This precut, compact sauna offers welcome relaxation in a minimum of space; an electric stove provides dry heat.

1 HOT TUBS AND SPAS

Communal bathing in heated waters has been popular since antiquity, even though Americans have only discovered its benefits in recent years. The Romans, Greeks, and Turks made public bathing a natural part of their lifestyles centuries ago, and the Japanese have retained this age-old custom into modern times. In America, however, most bathing in thermal waters prior to the last twenty years was restricted to the few natural settings where hot springs bubbled up from deep wells within the earth. Finally, in the late 1960s, bathing enthusiasts in the canyons around Santa Barbara, California, decided to make thermal water-bathing pleasures more accessible by introducing what has become known as the hot tub. The original California tubs were used wine vats rigged up with pipes, pumps, and heaters.

For those who desire a more luxurious, convenient, and versatile bathing experience, the fiberglass spa offers the same benefits as a hot tub without the rustic quality of wood. Molded fiberglass spas, which come in a wide variety of shapes, sizes, and colors, can satisfy almost any home design specification. They are also easier to maintain.

In spite of their differences spas and hot tubs perform basically the same function and operate in similar fashions. Both contain water heated to about 100 degrees Fahrenheit for adults (about 96 degrees for children). A pump circulates the water through a filter and heating system. Hydrojets may be added to increase the bubbling action.

Spas and hot tubs can be installed indoors or out, above ground or below. They can be attached to swimming pools or located on decks, patios, or rooftops. They are cheaper than swimming pools, occupy less space, use less water, and are far simpler to install yourself. Even though they require higher temperatures than heated pools, operating and maintenance costs are lower.

Spas are higher priced than hot tubs, although their operating and chemical maintenance costs are similar. Heat loss, however, is greater for a spa than a hot tub. A hot tub installed above ground and with an insulated cover will lose about 10 degrees Fahrenheit in 24 hours. A partially above-ground spa without special insulation will lose about twice that much heat. A comfort feature of spas that hot tubs don't enjoy is the option of molded seats, even reclining ones, while in hot tubs the seats tend to be upright. On the plus side, wooden tubs are much more portable than spas.

Although some claims concerning the benefits of thermal waters are over-inflated, spas and hot tubs are good for the mind and the body. Advocates of hydrotherapy point out that physical relaxation and psychological well-being are intimately related. Relaxed muscles and reduced stress levels are beneficial for high blood pressure, ulcers, and nervous disorders as well as for arthritis and other bone or joint ailments. Certainly it is a laudable goal to reduce stress and eliminate tension whenever possible. To enjoy the heat and massage of rapidly bubbling water with friends or family is a pleasant, sociable way to unwind and promote physical and mental fitness.

Certain precautions do need to be taken. People with heart ailments or circulatory problems should not engage in prolonged bathing, as the heat dilates veins, and less oxygenated blood returns to the heart and reaches the brain. Pregnant women, the overweight, and diabetics should consult a doctor before bathing; and alcohol and thermal waters don't mix. Always take a cool shower afterward to let your body temperature return to normal.

Hot Tubs: Basics and Types

The basic hot tub is made of wood according to traditional coopering methods. Beveled staves are attached to a solid wooden floor by means of a croze notch, also called a dado joint. The staves themselves are held in place by rustproof metal hoops. Each stave should be at least 1⅝ inches thick. Thicker staves retain heat better than thin ones. Inside the tub are attached wooden seats or benches that allow individual bathers to submerge most of their bodies in the water. The entire tub rests on pressure-resistant wooden joists that distribute the weight evenly.

The average hot tub is approximately 4 feet deep and 5 to 6 feet in diameter, which seats four to five adults comfortably. Some tubs, however, are as shallow as 2½ feet and as deep as 5 feet. Very small tubs may be 3½ feet across, and extremely large ones that accommodate many bathers at one time may reach 12 feet across. A typical 4 × 5-foot tub holds about 500 gallons of water; and a 4 × 6-foot tub holds 700 gallons.

A hot tub full of water and bathers can weight 7,000 to 8,000 pounds, so it requires a very stable and level foundation. What type of foundation is best for you depends on the type of soil that will support the tub. (In many areas, local building codes must also be considered.) If the soil is primarily clay and therefore firm, a crushed stone or gravel foundation that is 10 to 12 inches thick may be all you need. If your soil is more loosely packed sand or loamy dirt, an equally deep foundation of reinforced concrete is essential. Most hot tubs rest directly on their foundations; but if a permanent and more secure placement is desired, the joists of the tub can be set across sunken concrete piers.

CHECKING WOOD QUALITY

For the many people who enjoy putting a hot tub together themselves, easy-to-build kits are available with prefabricated parts. A high-quality tub, however, requires well-milled wood. Check the quality of the wood before you accept a kit. Not all manufacturers offer the same quality of materials, so it's best to check with local people who own hot tubs to inquire about quality and ease of assembly.

Staves must be cut with vertical grain to ensure a maximum swell factor. As the wood absorbs water it expands, tightening the seams between the staves. A certain amount of leakage, called weeping, occurs; but if the water level is kept at its optimum, such leaking is minimal.

Wood should be cut from the center of the tree. This all-heart wood resists leakage best and holds up better than wood cut from the periphery of the trunk, where the wood is softer and more prone to splintering and decay.

The most popular types of wood for hot tubs are California redwood, cedar, oak, and teak. Because the first tubs were made from redwood, it holds a special place in most people's imagination, and as a material it is ideal for the use and conditions a hot tub must withstand. It is most resistant to decay, and weathers into a pleasant gray color. Cedar, on the other hand, resists chemical damage better than redwood. Oak looks great but is the quickest to show

BASIC HOT TUB CONSTRUCTION

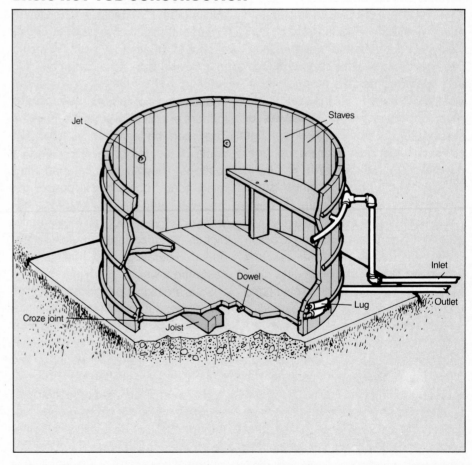

Hot tubs come in a range of sizes and shapes. The most common depths are 5 feet, 4 feet (shown above), and 2½ feet. In addition to the familiar straight-sided round tub, there are oval shapes and tubs with slanted sides.

signs of decay. Of all woods teak has the best qualities in terms of longevity and appearance but it is also the most expensive, and for this reason is not as popular as others.

Whichever type of wood you select, check to make sure the actual planks you purchase are free of defects such as knots, milling imperfections, and early signs of decay. All wood must be thoroughly seasoned, and kiln-drying rather than air-drying ensures that the wood will absorb moisture as evenly as possible. Wood that does not absorb moisture evenly can buckle or twist, separate at the seams, and cause serious leakage.

SETTING

A hot tub looks and functions perfectly well indoors, which may be the most logical setting for thermal water-bathing in a cold climate. The wood-iness of the tub makes it an attractively rustic focal point for a bathroom, family room, basement, greenhouse, or cabaña. Outdoor installation, however, is much simpler and more common. An outdoor hot tub will become a significant part of your overall landscape and should be specially framed to harmonize with the natural setting and the buildings around it. Most people choose to surround the hot tub with a floor of wooden decking, concrete, brick, stone, or patio blocks and then screen the entire area with privacy fences or shrubs.

Either wood or some type of masonry can provide an aesthetically appropriate surface next to a wooden hot tub; the final decision rests in which building material best suits the rest of the environment. An even more important consideration than aesthetics, however, is convenience and security. A customized tub-surround offers a safe, comfortable, and easy-to-maintain area for wet bathers to stand on when they emerge from the tub. A hot tub set simply onto a grass yard will be sitting in a mud puddle in no time. Care should therefore be taken to design the

HOT TUB SUPPORTS

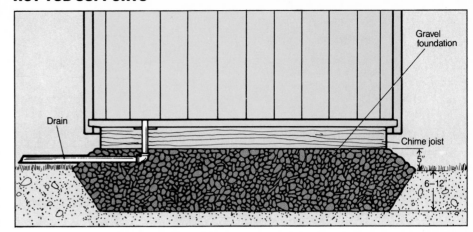

In a yard with firm soil, this gravel ballast-bed foundation rises partially above ground level to provide support for the chime joists beneath the tub floor. Note the drain that travels through the foundation.

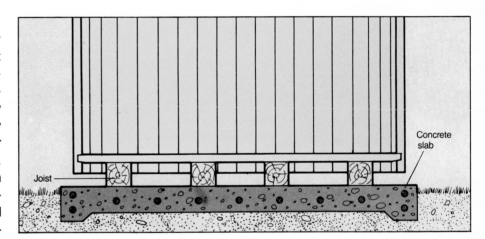

If you have a yard with relatively loose soil, or if you wish to make sure your tub foundation is stable, a reinforced concrete pad is the answer. The pad should extend beyond the perimeter of the tub and should be slightly thicker at its edges.

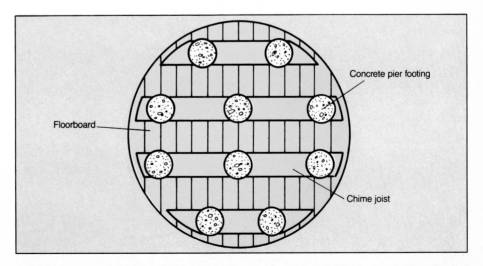

Concrete piers directly aligned with the chime joists provide ultimate stability for the tub. Once they are installed, however, they are difficult to remove; so be sure the tub is situated where you wish it to remain.

area that will surround the tub at the same time that you decide on the size and type of hot tub you want.

There are two major choices regarding the actual placement of the tub. The first is whether it will be installed below ground, that is, either sunk into an excavation cut out of the ground or with the top set flush with the floor of a wooden deck. The other is whether it will be installed in a free-standing position, either completely above ground or set on top of a deck.

A tub standing completely above ground becomes a focal point for the setting and should blend in well with plants, shrubbery, and other physical structures in the environment. It can be partially concealed by shrubbery or latticed fences if you don't want it to dominate the area. Without some kind of shelter, it will be exposed to such potentially damaging or uncomfortable elements as strong winds, dust, and, of course, intense sunlight. For maximum protection from winds, dust, and sun, create a high solid fence of wood or masonry to shield the tub, at least on the sides most likely to be affected. If you live in an area without harsh winds, a latticed or lath fence will block out the primary force of the wind while allowing for some soothing circulation of air.

A sunken hot tub is less obtrusive in a garden or yard or on a deck. It is also more protected from wind and harsh sunlight, and it retains heat better since it is less susceptible to fluctuations in the temperature.

A compromise between these two choices is to sink the tub halfway below the surface of the yard or a deck. If the deck has levels to begin with, you could incorporate the tub into one of the upper levels. This arrangement is the safest because it makes it less likely that people will fall into the tub, an easy thing to do near a tub flush with the ground level. At the same time, a tub sunk halfway is not as difficult to get into as one that is totally above ground. Usually a small stool or one step attached to the side of the tub, is all that is required to climb safely into it.

HOT TUB ENVIRONMENTS

This above-ground tub blends in with the surrounding deck area because it is made from the same type of wood, and the trees and shrubs provide a natural setting for it. Not only is it aesthetically pleasing, but the greenery provides privacy.

A hot tub partially sunk into a patio and surrounded at its lip by decking adds interest to the garden area and offers various levels for reclining and approaching the tub. Decking like this lets bathers sit on the edge of the tub.

Spas: Basics and Types

The first home spas were made of concrete or gunite. Using either of these materials, you can fashion an individual spa from scratch to fit its particular setting, although the shape of a concrete spa is generally restricted to straight lines and sharp angles due to the necessity of using wooden forms during the pouring process. In the early years of spa building, this kind of spa was usually attached to a swimming pool and mimicked the pool's design.

The advent of the hot tub inspired a whole new concept of spa usage and, therefore, of spa construction and design. A new emphasis was placed on spas that functioned independently from pools and were comfortable and easy to install and maintain. By far the most prevalent type of spa today consists of a fiberglass shell that has an inner lining of acrylic or gelcoat. These highly flexible materials let spa designers shape and mold extensive lines of spa shells to fit almost any situation, indoors or out. This is especially important to homeowners who have only a limited amount of space to devote to a thermal bathing unit or who wish to incorporate thermal bathing into an unusual design or landscape scheme.

The typical home spa, whatever its prefabricated shape, is approximately 4 feet deep and about 5 to 6 feet across, which holds four to six people comfortably, depending on the design. Most spas have sculpted seats and reclining areas, as opposed to traditional concrete or gunite spas, which feature flatter, more rigid resting surfaces. Concrete and gunite spas are frequently covered or lined with tile, and many people choose this style for its handsomeness, both indoors and outdoors; but the beauty and comfort of molded fiberglass make it an increasingly popular choice for spa material. Furthermore, fiberglass spas are fabricated in a variety of designer colors.

SPA CONSTRUCTION AND DESIGNS

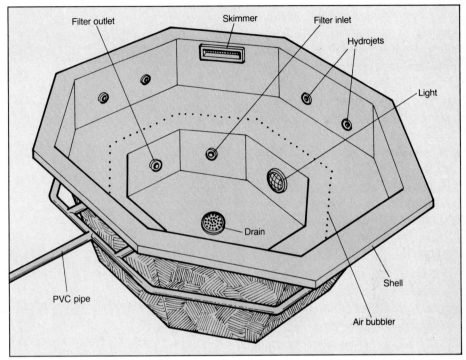

A typical fiberglass spa shell is made of layers of woven glass fiber and resin. Hydrojets pump heated aerated water into the tub at points on the side, and air bubblers spaced along the seating surface increase water turbulence.

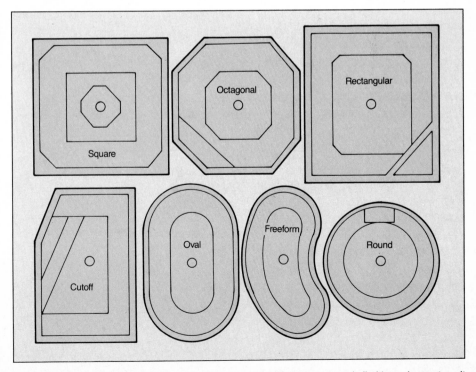

A major advantage of a prefabricated fiberglass spa is that this type comes in limitless shapes to suit space restrictions, design criteria, or personal desires: round, oval, square, rectangular, hexagonal, octagonal, cutaway, and free-style.

INSTALLING A FIBERGLASS SPA

The average home fiberglass spa as described above will weigh around 3,500 pounds when filled with water and people, so the support must be strong. For an indoor spa, consult an architect or engineer to make sure your floor can bear this weight. For an outdoor spa, you have numerous options to consider. The spa can be fully sunk into the ground, partially sunk into the ground, supported on ground level, or supported above ground level.

A fully sunken spa is more complicated to install than a hot tub, since it requires a larger, more supportive excavation. For most sites, the recommended mode of installation is known as the backfill method. This involves digging a pit 6 to 8 inches larger all around than the spa itself and then filling the space around the installed spa with sand that is wetted and compacted so that it can support the spa firmly at all points. In sites where the ground water is high or drainage is poor, the spa owner may need to build a concrete pad at the bottom of the pit and use heavy wooden beams to support the base of the spa.

A partially sunken spa requires a combination of a pit and retaining walls to hold compacted sand against all surfaces of the spa shell, including the portion above ground. This method works especially well when the spa is being placed on sloping land. It is simpler than creating a level surface big enough to support a fully sunken or above-ground installation, and it creates a convenient ledge from which bathers can enter and exit the finished spa.

An above-ground installation calls for thick retaining walls that take the place of the sides of a pit. If the ground soil is not fairly compact by nature, it may also require the placing of a concrete slab foundation on which wooden supports can be placed. Following this procedure, a spa can be raised to any above-ground height as long as a sturdy floor is constructed for the bot-

SPA INSTALLATION

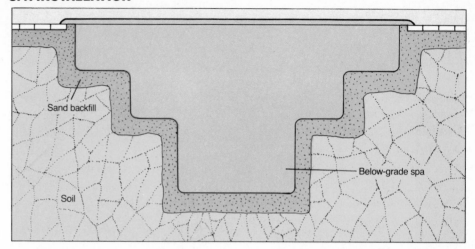

A sunken fiberglass spa should be placed in an excavation deep enough to allow room for the plumbing. The soil on all sides of the excavation should be well compacted. A bed of sand fills the space between the excavation and the shell.

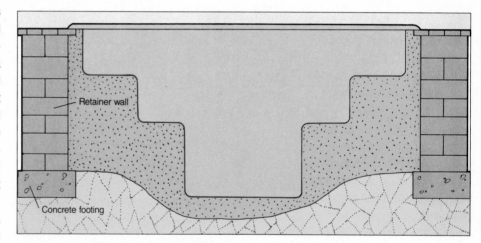

This partially sunken spa requires both an excavation and the erection of a sturdy masonry wall to support the lip of the shell rim. The wall can be trimmed in wood to achieve a more rustic look or to harmonize the spa with a wooden deck.

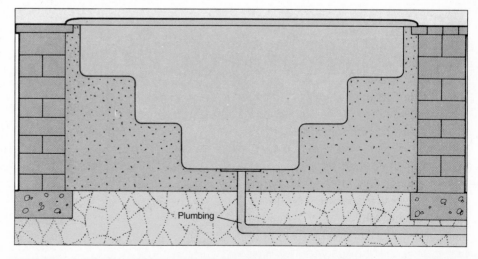

This above-ground spa installation requires a wall that is tall enough to hold the entire spa shell higher than the ground surface. If the spa is installed on a steep incline, a wall may be needed on only the downhill side.

tom of the artificial pit. It is in this manner that spas are incorporated into, or mounted on top of, raised decks.

CHOOSING A FIBERGLASS SHELL

The best way to select a spa is by the manufacturer's reputation and by checking with other owners for their comments on how satisfied they are with particular models and designs. Look for consistent thickness along the edges and be sure the surfaces are free of cracks, creases, or other blemishes. The thicker the shell is, the sturdier the spa is likely to be and the less heat loss it is likely to permit. Superior shells also have reinforcing ribs around seating areas and plumbing outlets.

There is considerable difference of opinion on whether an acrylic or gelcoat finish is better. Many people prefer acrylic, with its glossier colors, because it is a harder material and more resistant to abrasions and scratches, which are difficult to avoid with use. Acrylic is also quite resistant to chemical damage and can take high temperatures easily without damaging effect.

Gelcoat, on the other hand, is less expensive initially and is easier and cheaper to repair. It does require more maintenance than acrylic. As a finish, it is more susceptible to damage from sunlight and harsh chemicals. Colors tend to fade and the appearance is a duller, less brilliant color than acrylic.

CONCRETE AND GUNITE SPAS

For a more traditional-looking spa, gunite or concrete can be used. Building a gunite spa from the bottom up is a job requiring skill and expertise. First, the ground must be excavated and the plumbing laid in. Then a structure of steel webbing, molded to the desired shape of the spa, is installed. This is sprayed with gunite, which is a mixture of sand, cement, and water. When the gunite has hardened and the electrical hook-ups have been added, the interior is finished with plaster and a tile border

FIBERGLASS SPA MANUFACTURE

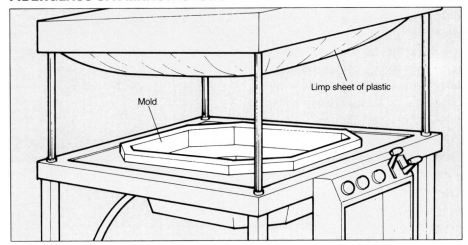

A fiberglass spa is manufactured by heating an acrylic sheet until it is soft enough to assume the shape of a mold.

GUNITE SPA INSTALLATION

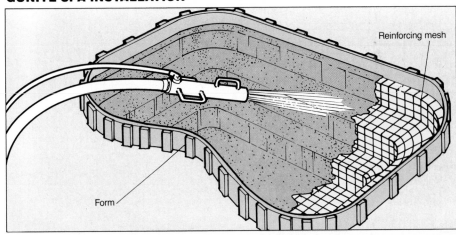

In terms of versatility of shape, a gunite spa lies between a fiberglass spa and a concrete spa. A steel web is fitted into an excavation and gunite is sprayed over the web.

CONCRETE SPA CONSTRUCTION

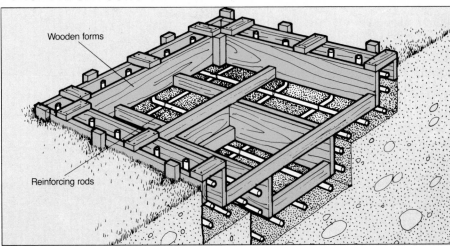

A concrete spa must be constructed with wooden forms, which limits the shapes that it can conveniently assume, since elaborate shapes are difficult to build with plywood and 2 × 4s.

added at the waterline. The inevitable "dirty ring" can be washed off tile more easily than from plaster.

A concrete spa is constructed in much the same fashion except that, because the concrete contains gravel, it must be poured over steel reinforcing rods rather than sprayed. Wooden forms are needed to shape and contain the concrete, so the variety of shapes is more limited.

In building a concrete or gunite spa, constant supervision is necessary to ensure quality control. The mixture must be uniform in quality to avoid weak areas that could eventually crack.

PORTABLE SPAS

A recent development in home spas is the portable fiberglass spa. Designed to be used either indoors or outdoors, the portable spa is ideal for people who move a lot or who live in rented homes. A compact unit only about 26 inches in depth fits through a standard-sized doorway and includes all the support equipment in a single assembly attached to the spa itself. It is installed above grade and enclosed in a skirting of wood or other attractive material to match the decor of its location.

One problem feature of some portable spas is getting the water hot and keeping it that way. The standard heater for portable spas is 1.5 kilowatts for a 110-volt system. It takes about 5 hours to raise 150 gallons 20 degrees Fahrenheit, so the capacity of the heater really limits the size of the spa to about 200 gallons. Often, maximum heat can only be maintained for about 20 minutes. Because of these limitations, potential purchasers of portable spas are advised to shop carefully and thoroughly.

PORTABLE SPA COMPONENTS

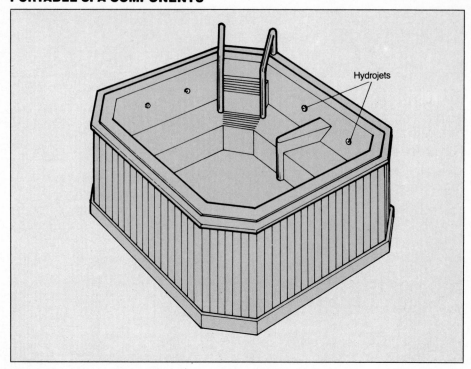

A portable spa usually comes with a built-in filter, jets, and electrical support system as well as an attractive skirt. It can seat from four to six people.

BATHTUB SPA SYSTEMS

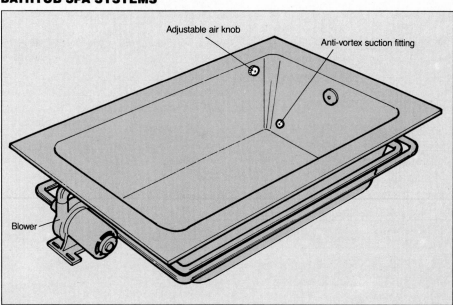

Some spa manufacturers produce hydrojet systems that can turn a conventional bathtub into a spa. They must be installed by professionals.

Support Equipment for Hot Tubs & Spas

The water used in hot tubs and spas is recirculated through a filter and a heater by means of a pump. Together the pump, the filter, and the heater make up the support system. They should be housed under a ventilated cover to protect them from the elements and to camouflage them, with at least 10 inches of space between the cover and the motor of the pump at all points. Their location should be less than 20 feet from the tub itself and close enough to utility lines for easy access.

The individual components of a support system can be bought separately or combined in what is called a skid pack. The problem with purchasing components separately is that they may not be compatible when they are finally linked together. A pump with a capacity that is significantly greater or less than that of the heater and filter won't work.

The advantage of a skid pack is that it is preplumbed and factory-tested to ensure that the individual parts are electrically and hydraulically matched. A good skid pack will service a tub or spa with a capacity of up to 600 gallons. It will cost more than you'd pay if you bought individual units, but for most spa owners the peace of mind that comes with not having to match parts is worth the extra expense. Installation is a simple matter of hooking up two or three plumbing lines to outlets in the tub or spa shell.

For larger spas and for greater flexibility in laying out the support equipment, individual components, carefully matched, need to be used. The advantage to this method of assembling a support system is that you can easily replace original components with larger or better ones as specific parts deteriorate, as your needs change, or as the technology advances.

Whether you buy a skid pack or not, you'll need at least two plumbing lines running between the spa and the support equipment: one line (called the suction line) to draw water out of the tub and into the filtering and heating system and the other line (called the return line) to pump water through the filtering and heating system and back into the tub. If an air blower is part of your support system (to increase water turbulence), a third line will be needed to conduct air to bubbler spouts or rings in the tub or spa shell.

SUPPORT SYSTEM COMPONENTS

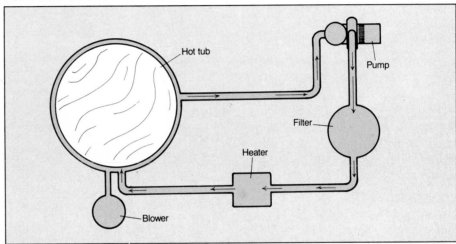

This diagram shows the basic components of a hot tub or spa support system. The plumbing layout recirculates hot, filtered water back to the tub instead of draining it away. All parts must be matched in size and power for smooth running.

SKID PACK SUPPORT SYSTEMS

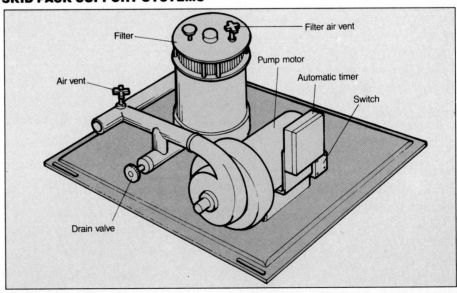

A skid pack is a preplumbed support system mounted on a pallet. This ensures that all parts match each other; a pack is easy to hook up by following the manufacturer's instructions. Skid packs come in different sizes and power ratings.

THE PUMP

The pump is the primary mover that sucks used water out of the tub and circulates it through the filtering and heating units. A ¾- to 2-horsepower centrifugal pump will handle most home spas. The actual size should be discussed with your dealer, since it depends on the size of the tub, the diameter of the pipes, whether the pump must also operate hydrojets, and where the support equipment is placed relative to the tub or spa shell.

The basic options are a one-speed pump, a two-speed pump, or two separate pumps. The two-speed pump is more energy-efficient than a one-speed pump because the high speed (about 3,500 rpms) used to operate hydrojets can be shut down to a lower speed when the jet action is not wanted. At the lower speed water will circulate more calmly. Two separate pumps achieve the same effect, one to operate the jets, the other to circulate water.

Originally pumps were made of brass and bronze, but in recent years different grades of plastic have proven viable. In fact, the plastic models are the most popular for home spas. The major concerns with plastic are to prevent them from freezing in winter or overheating. The difference in price among the various brands of plastic pumps reflects the quality of the plastic: the more durable the plastic, the more it costs. Pumps made of Noryl are quite reliable. Bronze and brass pumps usually last much longer, but are far more expensive.

FILTERS

There are three types of filters, all of which accomplish the same goal—namely, removing solid waste, dirt, algae, and other residue that accumulate.

The cartridge filter is the most widely used type of filter in home spas. Made with a rigid frame that supports a liner of nonwoven polyester, dacron, or a treated paper, the cartridge filter lets water pass through it while it traps foreign matter. Periodic cleaning is easily

SUPPORT SYSTEM PLUMBING

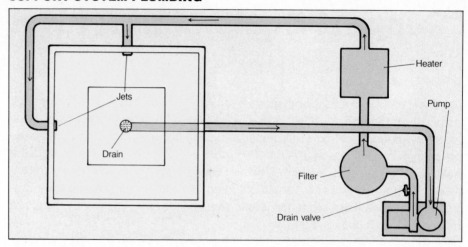

The standard support system consists of a pump, filter, and heater that recirculate water through two hydrojets. The longer the distance from the pump to the tub and the higher the water must be pumped, the lower the flow capacity.

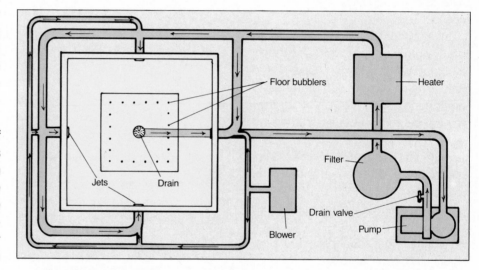

A more complex system incorporates a separate blower to accommodate additional jets. Its action intensifies the movement of the water and may allow you to get by with a smaller pump. But it also speeds up heat loss so you may need a faster heater.

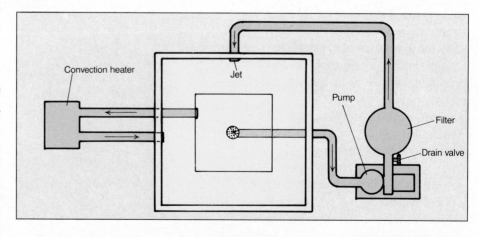

The simplest arrangement is a small pump linked to one jet. A convection heater operating on a separate power loop warms the water and pumps it back into the tub. This system has minimal water action but is much less expensive than the previous two.

done by removing the cartridge and washing it down with a garden hose. Many cartridge systems accommodate multiple filters to ensure that large volumes of water are adequately processed. Although cartridge filters do not sift out residue as finely as other types of filters, they do provide good water quality at a low price.

DE filters use diatomaceous earth, a very fine chalky substance that catches debris. Water pressure forces the DE against permeable plates. The water passes through the DE and the plate, leaving solid matter caught in the DE. These filters are more efficient than cartridges and can carry a heavier load of dirt. Because they provide an extremely tight system, they are used in commercial tubs and pools. Some homeowners use DE filters for large spas. When dirty, a DE filter is cleaned by reverse-flow backwash, after which a new coating of DE is added. This process uses some of the tub water, which is then discarded as waste. If you are considering this type of filter, check the amount of water lost and be sure your installation can handle the waste overflow.

Sand filters work like DE filters but use a hard-surface silica instead of DE. The filtration is not quite as tight as that of a DE filter, but most sand filters are slightly less expensive.

HEATERS

Heaters are powered by either fossil fuel (such as natural gas or propane), electricity, or solar power. Make your determination about which type of power to use based on heating costs in your area and on how fast you want the water to heat.

There are two types of fossil fuel heaters: the flash heater and the tank heater. The flash heater, also called the coil heater, produces a flame that heats a heat exchanger with one or two copper tubes. Fins on the tubes transfer heat to the water. Flash heaters are extremely efficient, providing heat quickly and maintaining a constant temperature. Keep in mind that a large-

sized flash heater will heat water more quickly than a smaller one but it uses the same amount of fuel. If you plan to turn your heater off when the tub is not in use, a large heater is recommended so that water can be brought to the desired temperature more rapidly.

The tank heater uses an open flame powered by a fossil fuel to heat a tank of water, similar to the standard hot water heater in most homes. Because the heat-up time is rather slow, the tank heater is usually not used for hot tubs or spas.

SPA WATER HEATERS

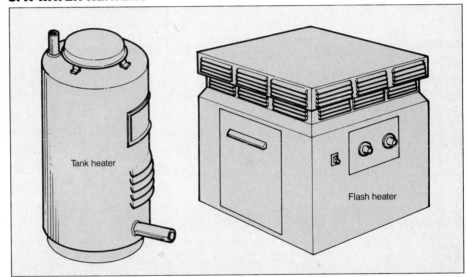

Gas heaters for spas come in two formats: flash heaters and tank heaters. Flash heaters, which are fed by an airflow, are far more practical because of their short recovery period.

The electric heater is used most often in skid packs. The heat output is less than that of a gas heater, so the heat-up time is much longer. Electric heaters are, however, adequate for small spas in which the water is left constantly heated. Their major disadvantage is the high cost of electricity. A 6-kilowatt heater can service a spa holding less than 300 gallons of water; a 12-kilowatt heater should be used for capacities up to 500 gallons. Most heaters are wired for 220-volt electrical systems.

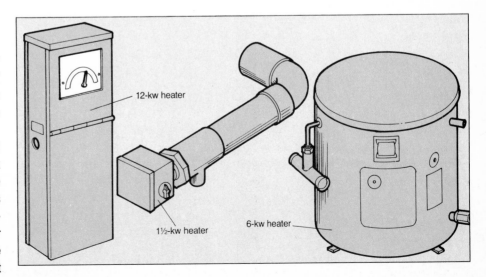

Electric heaters are the best choice for spas because of their compact size and fuel efficiency. If the spa is used regularly, the heater is kept running constantly to keep the water warm.

A solar heater is excellent for spas or tubs in sunny areas; but (as is always the case with solar heating), you'll need another heater as a backup if you want a dependable system.

The cover for your tub or spa should be considered an integral component of the heating system. If used properly and consistently, it can reduce the load on the heater up to half or more. Covers are either rigid or pliable. Wood or fiberglass make sturdy covers that are safe for small children to crawl over. Flexible insulated blankets are efficient but will not support any weight.

PURIFICATION SYSTEMS

Many spa and hot tub owners add a separate purification system to the basic support equipment to supplement the hygienic action of chemical purifiers. Since the water in a tub or spa is recirculated, it must be kept clean to combat infection and disease.

Three basic types of purifiers can be used as backups but not as substitutes for chemical additives, since they have no residual germ-killing action, nor do they immediately kill germs that enter the tub or spa while it is in use. These types are the ultraviolet sterilizer, the ionizer, and the ozone generator.

An ultraviolet water sterilizer causes microorganisms to explode. It consists of an ultraviolet bulb encased in a protective cover that is placed inside the circulating water. The ionizer uses electrical current running through metal electrodes to produce ions that kill organisms, which are then removed by the filter. The ozone generator converts oxygen in the air into ozone, then diffuses it through the water, thereby sterilizing the water before it reenters the tub or spa. Talk over the relative merits and costs of these extra purification systems with your dealer.

BLOWERS

Many bathers enjoy water that bubbles more rapidly and forcefully than water stirred by the action of a pump alone. In this case, a blower is added to the support system to give the pump a boost.

The original inventors of hot tubs in California are said to have used a vacuum cleaner running in reverse to agitate the water. Today there are safer and more efficient methods.

A very popular device for creating water turbulence is the venturi jet, sometimes called simply a hydrojet. It increases the velocity of the water flow by decreasing the diameter of the pipe through which it must pass. When water is forced through a constricted orifice at a given rate, the flow is speeded up. The process creates a vacuum that sucks in air that mixes with the water. The result is a rather fierce spew of water and bubbles that is dis-

charged through a hole in the side of the tub. Some holes have swivel spouts that can send the activated water in various directions.

Most authorities recommend the bypass blower, even though it is more expensive than the flow-through blower. The overall performance is better, and it is not as prone to water damage or overheating since it has a separate fan to cool the motor.

The pump on a blower should be located at least 12 inches above the water level if it is not protected by check valves and air loops. A bather blocking the bubbler could cause water to back up into the motor and ruin it.

HYDROJET COMPONENTS

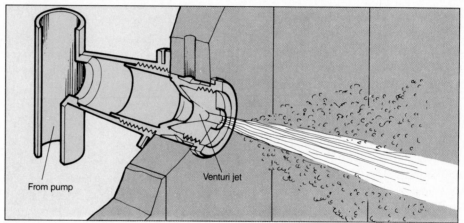

From pump   Venturi jet

The popular venturi jet, or hydrojet, makes bathing in a hot tub or spa an invigorating experience. Water pumped through it accelerates as the diameter of the orifice shrinks. Swivel spouts direct the stream away from the body.

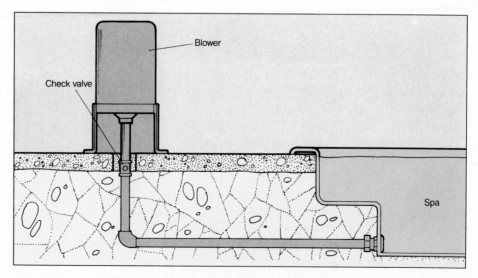

Blower
Check valve
Spa

To prevent water from backflowing into the blower, a check valve is installed on the blower line near the blower itself. The check valve should be at least 2 feet above the waterline.

Site Orientation

Choosing a site for your hot tub or spa can be fun and creative. Every yard has several options, and determining which is best for your needs can be an adventure in landscaping your property so that your design meets both aesthetic and practical requirements.

On a piece of graph paper draw a scale model of your property, including all buildings, trees, shrubs, walks, and other structures. Sketch the path of the sun as it makes its way across the sky each season, noting where the shadows fall at different times of the day. Take into account the prevailing wind currents. Mark utility connections. Note setback boundaries and height limitations. Consider areas that provide the most privacy and yet offer a pleasant view.

Then, on a piece of tracing paper placed over your scale drawing, sketch out the various options. Keep in mind the following guidelines. Your unit should:

● Be near enough to the main house for comfortable use

● Be near enough to utility lines to avoid the added expense of running them out to the site

● Have enough privacy for nude bathing

PLANNING RECREATIONAL INSTALLATIONS

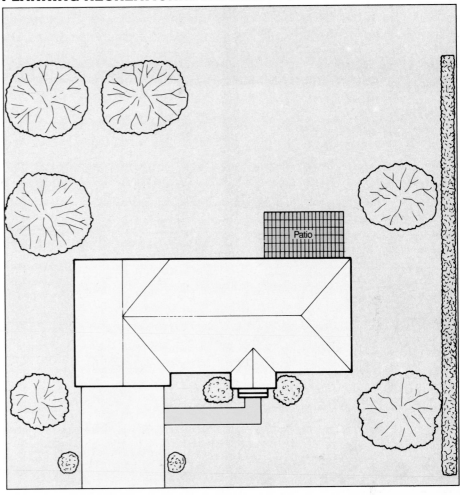

Begin planning your hot tub/spa installation by making a scale drawing of your home, the surrounding trees and shrubs, and the total area of your property available for recreational installations. Indicate the seasonal shifts of sun and shade as shown below.

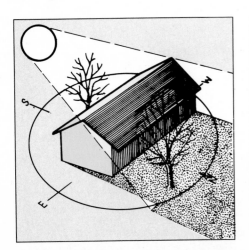

During winter months in most of the U.S., the sun remains low in the sky at noon, casting long shadows on the opposite side of the house.

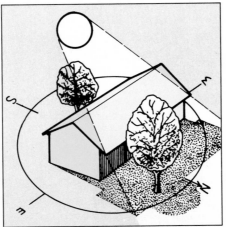

During the spring and fall, the sun is about half-way between its lowest and highest points; moderate shade is cast.

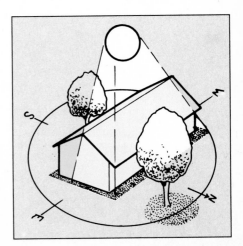

During the summer, with the sun at its highest point, very little shade is created; you may have to make your own with trees or a roof.

● Provide a pleasant view

● Be in a location that utilizes the best daylight hours and takes the wind factor into account

● Be away from trees or shrubs that would drop leaves

● Be situated so that runoff will flow away from the unit rather than into it.

If you plan to have a full enclosure for your tub or spa (either as a free-standing unit or attached to the house), you'll be able to use it year-round. Some units are prefab and easy to assemble. You'll also reduce heat and chemical costs since windows will capture heat and keep dirt out of the water. You might consider making it large enough to accommodate a greenhouse, since fully enclosed tubs create a lot of water vapor. An enclosed spa is ventilated by windows, air vents, and exhaust fans, or a combination of these. Depending on your climate, you may need to eliminate excess humidity.

CREATING VARIATIONS IN RECREATIONAL FACILITIES

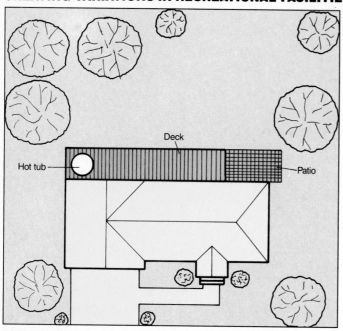

A first step in adding to your outdoor facilities might be to build a deck from the patio across the width of your house, with a hot tub/spa in one corner.

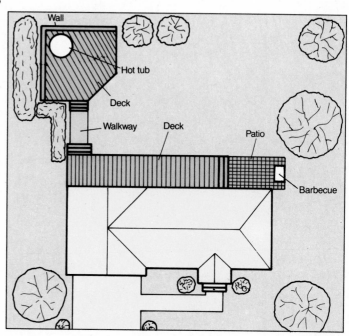

The next step might include building a second deck in a sheltered corner and a barbecue pit on the patio.

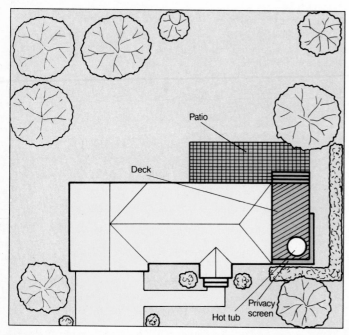

If the rear of your property is not inviting, build a deck around the opposite corner, and if necessary, screen it with a hedge or solid wall.

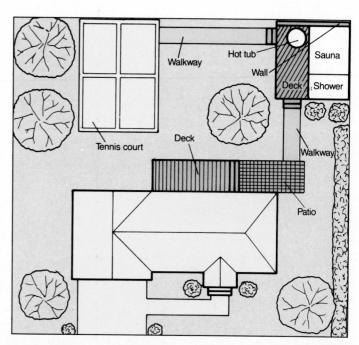

This plan fills the entire property with recreational opportunities, including a deck, tennis court, and hot tub/spa combined with a sauna in the far corner.

ADAPTING FACILITIES TO LOT RESTRICTIONS

On a restricted site, where the hot tub/spa must be tucked away in a corner, a long, curving flagstone path seems to extend the dimensions (right). On an odd-shaped, exposed lot (below left) the hot tub/spa and its deck retreat into a corner of the house for privacy. A bit of lawn near the street provides contrast. A narrow lot (below right) will seem less restricted if the hot tub/spa and deck are separated from house and lawn by a curving path, shrubs, and perhaps a slight elevation.

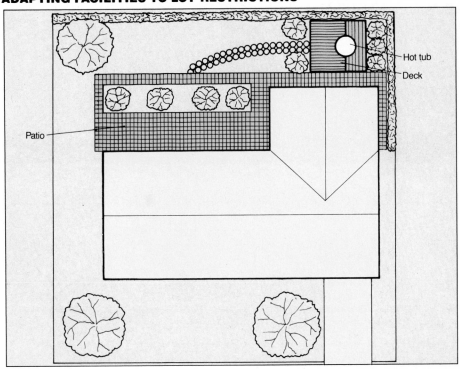

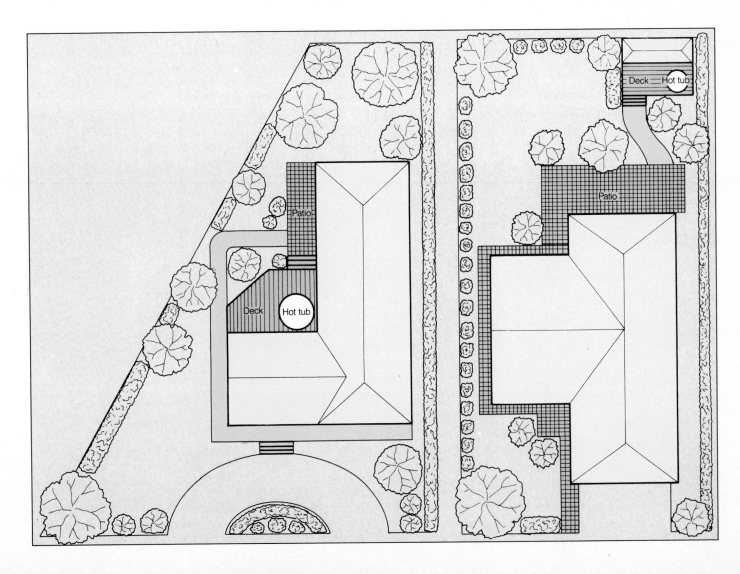

AN UNRESTRICTED OUTLOOK

If your hot tub/spa looks out over splendid scenery, make the most of it by leaving the installation completely open.

A LIGHT-WEIGHT SHELTER

If you prefer some shade and shelter, an open trellis provides both without cutting off breezes and light completely.

A TRANSPARENT WINDBREAK

Glass walls are one solution for a deck that is swept by winds. The view remains unhindered, while the doors can be opened on still days.

A LOUVERED PRIVACY WALL

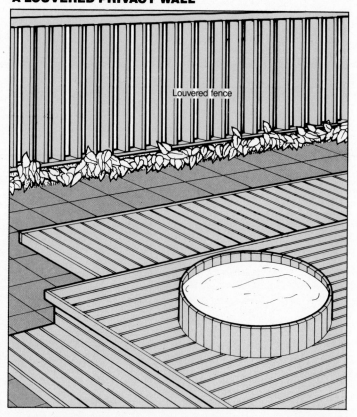

Louvered fence

If you require visual privacy, a louvered wall is the answer. Air circulation is not hindered; the wall will support vines to break up its rigid lines.

Installing a Hot Tub Step-by-Step

A wooden deck encircling an outdoor hot tub can provide a pleasant and efficient environment for bathing and relaxing, whether you are enjoying some time alone or entertaining guests. The soft, weathered wood provides an excellent floor around the tub—comfortable for bare feet, easy to keep clean, and aesthetically in harmony with the lines and materials of the tub itself. A typical wooden deck also has spaces between the floorboards that allow water spilled from the tub to drain through to the ground below. The major benefit of a wooden deck around a tub is that the immediate area bordering

the tub is free from mud and dirt.

As for the design of your deck-and-tub layout, several options present themselves. You can have a hot tub literally sitting on the floor of a wooden deck, as long as the weight of the finished tub, including water and bathers, complies with the weight regulations in your local building code. For easier access, you may prefer a tub completely surrounded by the surface of the deck and flush with the floor, or a tub that sits in a bay at the edge of the deck. Finally, you may choose the drama and versatility of a more elaborate structure, such as a multilevel deck, with some

levels acting as landings that lead up to the top of the tub.

The hot tub installation project that follows features a deck attached to the wall of the house and partially enclosing a hot tub (see below for design). The top rim of the hot tub is sunk flush with the floor of the deck—not only to provide easy access to the tub itself, but also to prevent the tub from obscuring views from the house or deck. Before implementing this project on your own property, check the sections of your local code that pertain to attached structures, weight regulations, and footing sizes.

PLAN OF HOT TUB AND DECK PROJECT

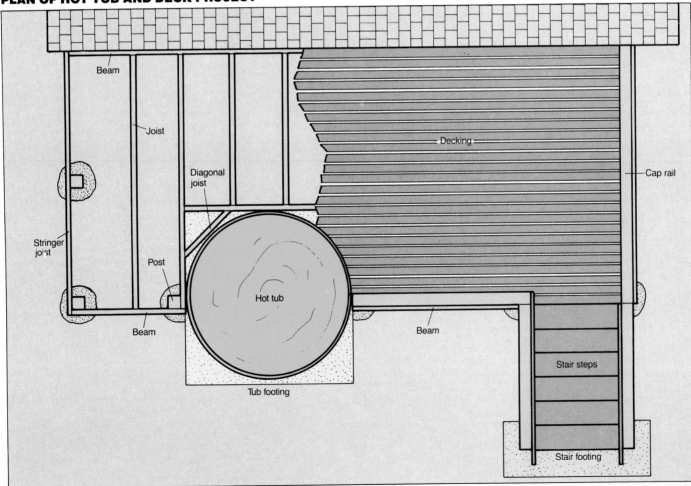

A hot tub and raised deck can turn a rocky or uneven yard into an exciting recreation area. If the ground slopes away from the house, you'll have no problem with drainage. Check with building authorities for joist specifications.

STEP 1
PREPARING THE SITE

Remove all plants, shrubs, rocks, and sod in the area the deck will cover. Make sure the ground below the deck slopes slightly as it goes away from the house. After you stake out the corners of the deck using a triangulated survey method, you are ready to begin the project (see page 108).

STEP 2
PLACING A CONCRETE SLAB

For maximum stability, the tub must sit either on a concrete slab or on piers sunk in concrete footings (see below). If a concrete slab is sufficient for your purposes, begin by digging a foundation bed approximately 9 inches deep and 6 inches longer and wider than the circumference of the tub. Fill the bottom 5 inches of the bed with gravel, then lay a wire mesh on top of the gravel for reinforcement. Pour about 4 inches of concrete on top of the mesh. Set the end of the slab away from the house ½ inch to 1 inch lower to create a slope for draining.

STEP 3
INSTALLING PIER FOOTINGS

If you desire a more permanent installation, you may want to use piers sunk into concrete footings. Piers can be either concrete cylinders or pressure-treated wooden posts. How many piers you should use and how they should be spaced in relation to the chime joists depends on the specific hot tub you have purchased, so follow your dealer's suggestion. The footing itself should rest only on solid, well-drained ground. The tops of the piers should be level across joists and slope ½ inch to 1 inch away from the house lengthwise along joists for draining.

STEP 4
PLACING THE CHIME JOISTS

The chime joists that support the floor of the tub can rest freely upon a concrete slab foundation without any secondary attachment. The substantial weight of the tub will hold them in place.

LAYING A CONCRETE PAD FOUNDATION

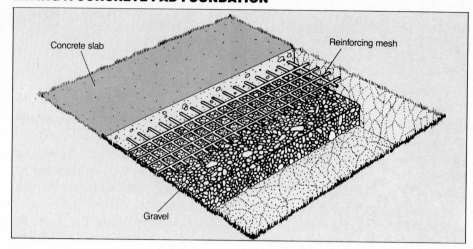

This concrete pad foundation, consisting of a 6-inch gravel layer topped by a reinforced 5-inch concrete layer, provides dependable stability in most climates. If winters are very cold, each layer may have to be proportionately thicker to prevent cracking.

INSTALLING CONCRETE PIER FOOTINGS

1. Concrete pier footings provide foundation stability in areas with loose soil or severe climate. Placement must be made exactly according to tub dealer specifications, based on the location of the chime joists.

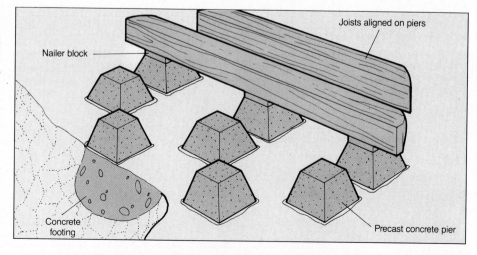

2. If you have a concrete pier foundation, set a nailer block on top of each pier to act as a buffer between the pier itself and the chime joist. Then toenail the chime joist into the nailer block.

If you are using piers that have been sunk into concrete footings, the chime joists need to be toenailed to the wooden blocks on top of the piers. In either case, the chime joists must be level with each other and they must slope slightly lengthwise away from the house to make draining the tub easier.

STEP 5
FLOORBOARDS

Lay the floorboards beveled-side down and at right angles to the chime joists. Some hot tub kits number the boards sequentially, so check to see if the boards you are using have numbers anywhere on their surfaces. If so, rely on these numbers to determine the board placement. Set down the center boards first and alternate, adding a board to each side. Whether the boards in your kit have dowels or a tongue-and-groove system, tap each succeeding board gently with a mallet so that it fits snugly against the previous board.

STEP 6
SEATING THE STAVES

Mark a guideline around the edge of the floor equal to the depth of the croze. If the staves are predrilled for support equipment, place them where you want the support hookups to be. With an assistant, center the first stave and drive it half the depth of the croze line. Keep the staves at 90-degree angles to the floor. No stave should be seated fully at this point. Tightening the hoops later will seat them fully. Work clockwise, tapping each stave snug with its neighbor at the base. The tops of the staves may be out of line.

STEP 7
PREVENTING JOINT ALIGNMENT

As you are placing the staves around the floor, make sure that you do not place a stave joint less than ¼ inch from a floor joint. This type of juncture creates a structural weakness in the finished tub that more easily invites leakage. If you find that a stave joint aligns

INSTALLING FLOORBOARDS

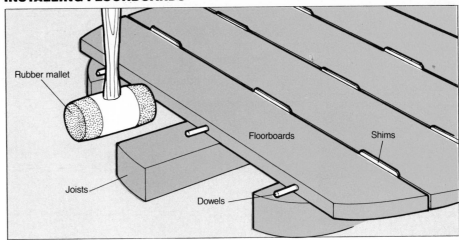

When the joists are level, arrange the floorboards on them in the correct order so they form a circular floor. Insert dowels in the predrilled holes. Put ¹⁄₁₆-inch shims between the boards to allow for swelling. Tap the boards together with a mallet.

INSTALLING STAVES

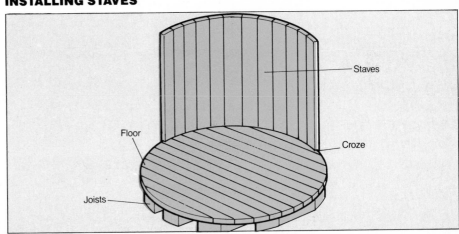

1. A guideline marked on the floor the depth of the croze joint will help you position the staves at first when they should be tapped in only half the depth of the croze. Work slowly in a clockwise direction, aligning each stave at the base with its neighbor.

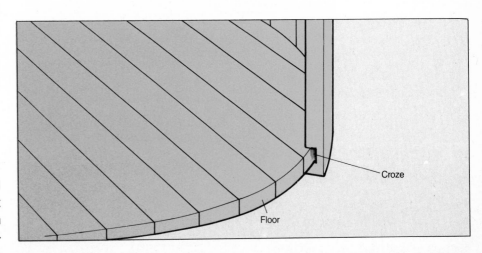

2. A joint between individual staves should never fall along a joint between floorboards or the chances of a leak are greatly enhanced. To correct such a joint misalignment you may have to readjust all the staves or trim the neighboring staves.

closely with a floor joint, stop and re-move the stave. Then work backward (counterclockwise). To prevent un-wanted joint alignment, trim the last two staves so that they are thinner; the other staves will shift position.

STEP 8
FITTING THE LAST STAVE
If the last stave doesn't fit, you will have to trim it with a plane or have it milled. Measure the gap between the first stave and the second-to-last one. Use a T-bevel on each stave to determine the angle of the bevel on each side of the final stave. If you have kept the wood warm and dry (approximately the same condition as when it left the man-ufacturer), you will probably not have any trouble making the last stave fit.

STEP 9
ATTACHING THE HOOPS
With an assistant, attach the first hoop at the bottom, centering it on the edge of the floor. Use small nails every six or seven staves to hold the hoop in place while you work on it. Remove the nails after it is completely tightened. Center the first lug over a stave joint. Tighten just enough to hold the hoop in place, then add other hoops according to manufacturer's instructions, usually with the second hoop lug placed on the opposite side of the tub. Stagger the lugs over different stave joints.

STEP 10
TIGHTENING THE STAVES
Beginning with the bottom hoop and working up, tighten the lugs so that each hoop is snug against the staves. Be sure to allow the staves to remain seated at half the croze depth. One person tightens the lugs while the other gets in the tub and hammers the sides of the staves with a rubber mallet so that they form a smooth, round inside. Perform this routine six or seven times until the staves are seated flush with each other and with the edge of the floor as indicated by the guideline. To ensure a watertight tub, all seams must be extremely close-fitting.

INSTALLING STAVES (CONTINUED)

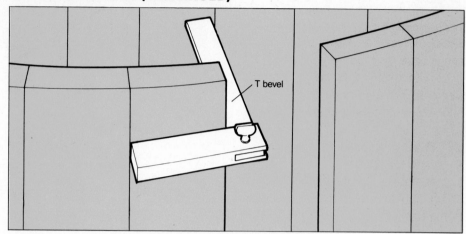

3. Changes in temperature and humidity may swell staves after they have been cut by the manufac-turer. If such is the case, you may have to trim the last stave to fit. Use a T-bevel to determine the correct angle for each side of the final stave.

INSTALLING HOOPS

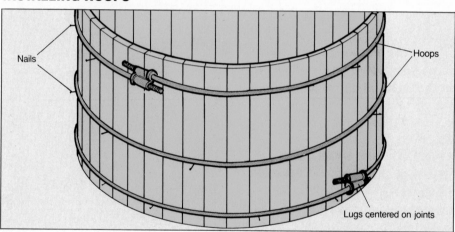

1. When positioning the hoops, begin at the floor level and place the lugs over adjoining stave joints. Stagger the lugs so that they are not all on one side of the tub. Small nails driven under the hoop every few staves will hold it in place until it is tightened.

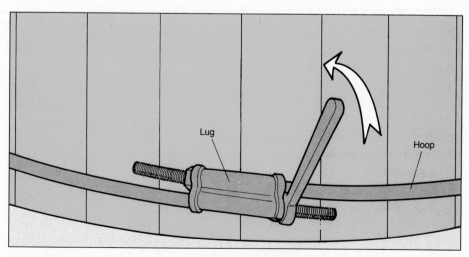

2. Take your time in tightening the hoops so that the staves are pulled into position gradually to form a smooth interior. The guideline marked on the floor at the depth of the croze cut shows at what point the staves are completely seated.

STEP 11
CONNECTING THE SUPPORT SYSTEM

Install each component of your support system according to dealer's instructions. (See page 47 for more detailed instructions.)

STEP 12
SEASONING THE TUB

Fill and drain the tub several times over the next few days to allow the wood to swell. Reddish water caused by tannin indicates the wood is leaching. This is not considered a health hazard and will stop in about three months. If a serious leak occurs, do not try to correct it by tightening the lugs. Instead, loosen the lugs one or two turns and, starting on the side opposite the leak, hammer the sides of the staves, doing two on each side and alternating sides until you work your way back to the leak. Repeat as necessary.

STEP 13
ATTACHING THE HOUSE-SIDE DECK BEAM

Now it's time to attach the first beam(s) of the deck to the house. Be sure that the top edge of the beam is 1½ inches lower than the height of the finished deck to allow for the thickness of the planks. Drill ½-inch bolt holes at 12-inch intervals along the center of the beam. For a wooden wall, use ½-inch lag bolts, 6 inches long. For a cinder-block wall, use 14-inch lengths of ½-inch threaded rod with nuts and washers on each end and back blocks 8 inches long cut from 2 × 8 lumber. For a brick or concrete wall, drill ¾-inch holes and use ½-inch lag bolts, 6 inches long, inserted into lead expansion shields.

STEP 14
SETTING UP THE OUTSIDE DECK BEAM

After you have finished attaching the first beam(s) of the deck to the house, dig post holes at least 18 inches deep in which to place the support posts for the outside edge of the deck. Pour con-

COPING WITH LEAKS

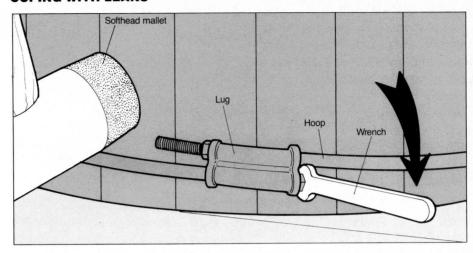

If a serious leak develops once the lugs are tightened, do not try to force the staves by further tightening. Instead, loosen the lugs and tap the sides of the staves with a rubber mallet.

CONSTRUCTING THE DECK

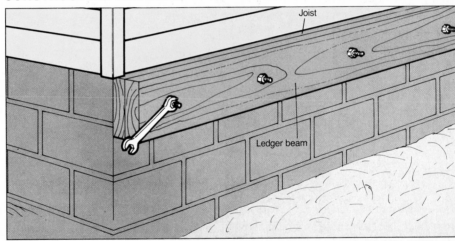

1. A deck attached to a house must be firmly secured to a ledger beam the same size as the joists bolted to the side of the house. Cut the beam to the desired length and attach it 1½ inches lower than the height of the deck to allow for the deck flooring.

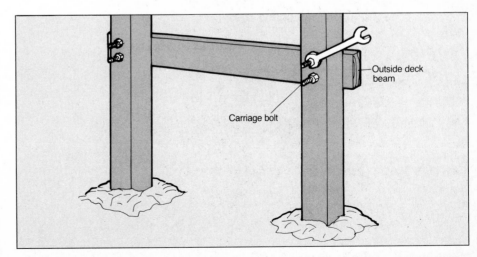

2. When attaching an outside deck beam to its posts, first nail it into place temporarily, with the beam in front of the post, facing outward toward the yard. Then drill ½-inch holes through both the post and the beam to make room for the carriage bolts.

crete into these holes (directly against the soil) and set the support posts in the wet concrete. Be sure that the posts are level and plumb. After the concrete has cured and the posts are securely set, attach the beam(s) for the front edge of the deck to these posts with two ½-inch carriage bolts, 6 inches long, on each post.

STEP 15
INSTALLING DECK JOISTS

Now that the house-side and outside beams are in place, connect the stringer joists that form the sides of the deck. Attach one end of the stringer joist to the outside of the corner support post with ½-inch carriage bolts (in the same manner that you attached the outside beam to the support posts). Fasten the other end of the stringer joist to the house-side beam(s) with steel framing connectors. Then mark the house-side and outside beams where the interior joists will join them and mount framing connectors at these locations. Insert the interior joists and nail them in place.

STEP 16
MAKING THE TUB BAY

To create a sturdy bay in the deck to enclose the hot tub, install framing connectors for hanging a header joist. The header joist will span the standard joists on each side of the bay. With the header joist firmly connected, attach a diagonal joist in each right angle formed by a standard joist and the header joist. The ends of these diagonal joists need to be cut at 45-degree angles to fit snugly against the other two joists. Secure the header joist with four 16-penny nails at each end.

STEP 17
LAYING THE DECKING

Begin with the plank against the house wall, using two 12-penny nails at each joist. Insert a piece of ¼-inch hardboard between each plank to allow space for air circulation and water drainage. Let the boards overlap the stringer joists at the end. Attach 2 × 4

CONSTRUCTING THE DECK (CONTINUED)

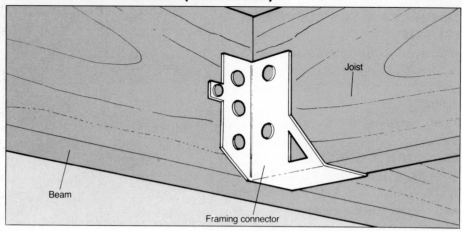

3. Steel framing connectors make it relatively easy to attach joists to the beams. Check with a local hardware store for the size and strength you will need. Mark where the joists meet the beams and attach the framing connectors to the beam. Then nail in joists.

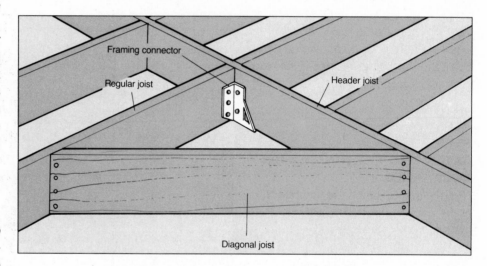

4. To make a bay in the deck to surround the hot tub, cut off the regular joists, according to the width of the tub, and connect them to a header joist. Then nail diagonal joists in the corners.

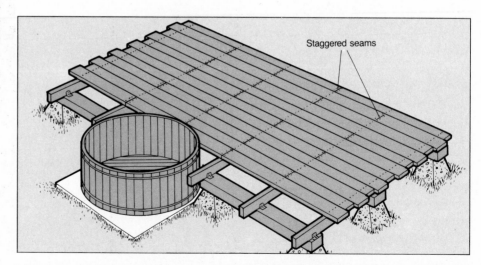

5. If you have to use more than one board to span the deck, cut the lengths so that the seam is over a joist, not between joists. To make the deck as solid as possible, stagger the seams so that they do not all fall over the same joists.

cleats to the support posts where the decking will meet them. Drill two ⅛-inch holes to keep the cleat from splitting when you nail it on with two 12-penny nails. The grain of the cleat should run horizontally. Lay the last board at the deck edge after installing the stair stringers (see page 40).

STEP 18
FINISHING THE DECK EDGE

The edge of the deck should be even and smooth, but probably at this point individual planks stick out at different lengths. When all but the last plank (facing the stairs) are in place, mark the true edge of the deck on each side. Draw a line across the ends of the planks with a pencil or chalk string. Then saw off the ends of all the planks with a single cut, carefully following the line you have drawn. Sand the cut ends until they are smooth and perfectly in line and then attach headers (or wooden trim) all around the deck perimeter. These headers will help prevent the ends of the planks from splitting and splintering.

STEP 19
MAKING IRREGULAR CUTS

Use a scriber to mark the curve of the tub on a board that meets it. If the curve falls on the end of a board, place it along the last board nailed down. One corner of the board will meet the wall of the tub. Place one point of the scriber against the tub, the other perpendicular to the board at its edge. Transfer the curve to the board by moving the scriber along the wall. For a curve along the edge of a board, place it on top of the last nailed board and slide it up to meet the tub, keeping both boards parallel. Set the scriber ¼ inch wider than the lip between the two boards. Place one point of the scriber perpendicular to the floorboard and the other against the tub. Move it along the tub to transfer the curve to the board.

STEP 20
PLACING THE STAIR FOOTING

Wet stairs are safer if they have wide

TRIMMING DECK BOARDS

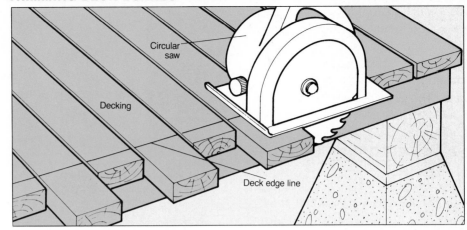

1. Use a circular power saw to cut off the irregular ends of the floorboards and make the deck edge smooth. Then you can attach headers around the deck edge. The edge of the deck should extend a few inches out from the perimeter beams as shown.

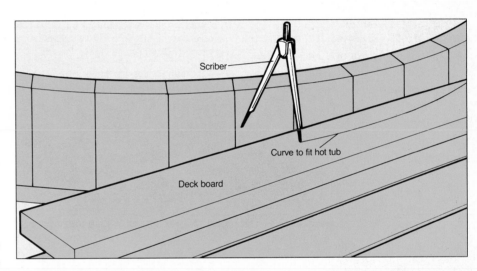

2. At a point where the deck meets the rounded edge of the tub, a curved cut will have to be made. Use a scriber to transfer the curve of the tub to the board to be cut. Before nailing down any irregular board, make a trial fit to be sure the board is the correct length.

INSTALLING THE STAIRS

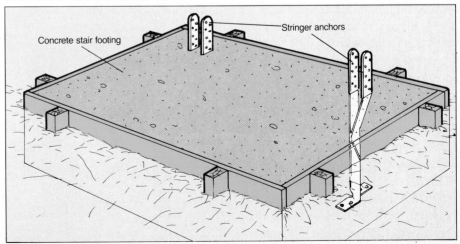

1. Dig a hole for the concrete stair footing that will reach below the frost line. The footing itself should be 3 to 4 feet from front to back. Lay it out so that the anchors for the stair stringers will be positioned about 1 foot from the back edge of the footing.

treads and short risers. Wide treads also make stairs that double as comfortable informal seating. To achieve this design, first position the anchors for the stair stringers as far away from the edge of the deck as the deck is high. The concrete footing should be about 3½ feet from front to back and about 1 foot wider than the stair width. The anchors should be set about 1 foot in from the back edge. Spread the wings of the anchors 1½ inches apart to fit the thickness of the stringers.

STEP 21
MAKING THE STAIR STRINGERS

Rest a 2 × 8 wooden beam on its edge against the deck, the opposite end resting on its corner about 4 inches beyond a framing anchor. This stringer should rise at about a 45° angle. Holding a level vertical at the top of the board and flush against the deck beam, draw a diagonal line along the level to mark the top cut. Keeping the board in position, mark a line along the level held vertical at the corner that rests on the footing near the anchors. Draw another line at a right angle to the first where it intersects the top edge of the stringer. This second line marks the bottom cut. Join the stringer to the deck beams with steel framing connectors.

STEP 22
ATTACHING THE CLEATS

To determine the number of treads on each stringer, measure in inches the vertical distance from the footing to the top of the deck. A plank extending out level from the deck can be used as a reference point. Divide this distance by the height you have chosen for risers. Round off the fraction to the nearest whole number and subtract 1 to give you the number of stair treads. Calculate the interval between cleats by dividing the vertical distance from the footing to top of deck by the number of treads plus 1. Mark these intervals on the stringer and attach the cleats 1½ inches below the mark. This will allow for the thickness of the tread.

INSTALLING THE STAIRS (CONTINUED)

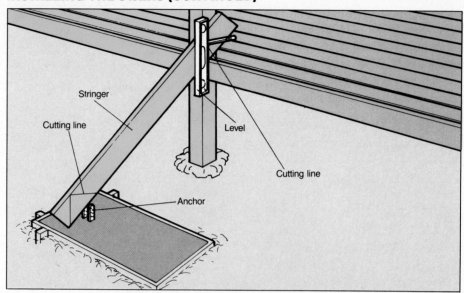

2. To mark the stringers, set a 2 × 8 against the deck and about 4 inches outside the anchors. Draw vertical lines near the top and from the bottom corner, as shown. Then draw a horizontal line at a right angle to the bottom vertical. Make the cuts. Cut a second stringer identical to the first.

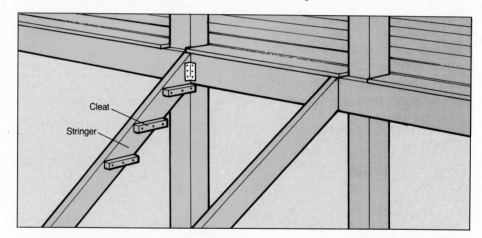

3. Stairs that rise at 45 degrees usually have 8-inch risers. Divide the distance from deck to footing by 8 and round off the result. Subtract 1 to get the number of treads. When positioning the tread cleats on the stringers, allow 1½ inches for the tread thickness.

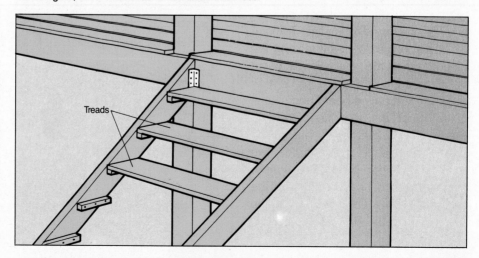

4. Nail the 2 × 3 cleats in place, checking to be sure they're level. Then attach the 2 × 10 treads. Begin at the top pair of cleats. To be safe, the treads must fit snugly between both stringers; make the outside edge of each tread flush with the top of both stringers.

STEP 23
ATTACHING THE TREADS

Once the cleats are in place, cut and attach the stair treads to them. First cut 2 × 10 wooden treads so that they will fit snugly between the stringers. Make sure there are no knots or structural deformities on these treadboards since they have to take more abuse than the decking itself. After you have set the treads in place, nail them to the cleats with 10-penny nails. Make sure that the outside edge of each tread winds up flush with the top edge of each stringer.

STEP 24
ATTACHING THE GUARDRAILS

Bolt a 4 × 4 post to the foot of each stringer. Cut all posts around the deck to a uniform height. Nail 2 × 4 wooden guardrails to the insides of the posts around the perimeter of the deck itself and on both sides of the stairs, placing one guardrail midway up the posts and the other flush with the tops of the posts. Then attach 2 × 6 cap rails. For greatest stability, the seams in the guardrails should fall at the posts. The seams in the cap rails should be made between the posts, rather than at the posts, to protect the top end grain of the posts from rain.

INSTALLING THE STAIRS (CONTINUED)

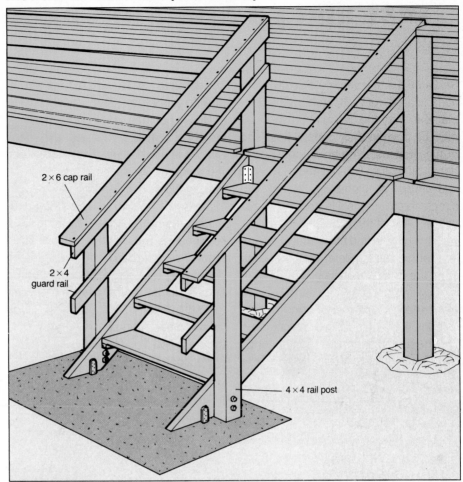

2 × 6 cap rail

2 × 4 guard rail

4 × 4 rail post

5. Cut the two 4 × 4 rail posts to the same height and bolt them to the stringer bottoms. Miter the four stair-rail post tops, using the same angle as for the stringers. This lets the guardrail and cap rails sit flush on the posts.

COMPLETED HOT TUB AND DECK PROJECT

Installing a Spa Step-by-Step

Because a spa is technologically more complicated than a hot tub, many people fear that the installation process may be beyond their capabilities. The truth is that installing an outdoor spa is not as difficult as it might seem. A basic knowledge of plumbing, along with simple excavating skills and a little patience, will get the job done.

Many people find that installing a spa by themselves is easier than installing a hot tub by themselves because there are fewer steps and pieces to assemble. In fact a spa installation involves just one large piece. On the other hand you must plan carefully, because once mistakes are made, they are harder to

correct than mistakes made when installing a hot tub.

Unlike hot tubs, spas come in a wide variety of shapes and sizes, with many options in site design. This means that the following instructions must, of necessity, be rather general.

Adding a spa to your property requires the appropriate building and electrical permits. There may be other regulations affecting your installation, depending on your local codes, so be sure to check thoroughly before committing yourself to any one plan. If you follow all code requirements right from the start, you won't have to make major corrections later.

The project outlined in the following pages calls for a below-grade spa installation in a brick patio, with support equipment located about 12-feet away (see plan below). This plan can be adapted to any type of outdoor below-grade installation.

In all spa installations there should be 10 to 15 feet between the spa shell itself and its support equipment, in order to ensure the most efficient operation. The pump should be below the spa water level so that it will be self-priming. If the heater inlet is more than 3 feet below water level, the pressure switch on the heater will have to be recalibrated.

PLAN OF A BELOW-GRADE, OUTDOOR SPA INSTALLATION

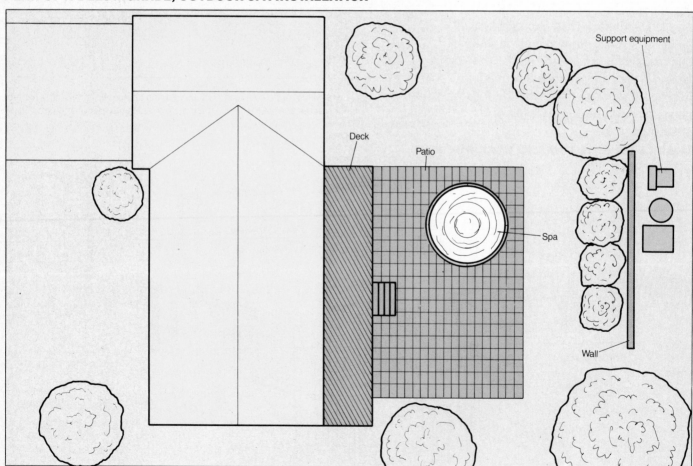

When building a below-grade spa in a backyard recreation area, place the support equipment between 10 and 15 feet away. In the plan above, the equipment is hidden at right behind shrubs and a sound deadening wall.

STEP 1
PREPARING AND GRADING THE SITE

When your site has been approved by the local building inspector, clear away all rocks, plants, and other obstructions. Check carefully for tree root systems that could interfere with plumbing or masonry work. Then grade the site so that there will be level ground on all sides of the spa equal to the depth of the spa below the ground. For example, if the bottom of the spa sits 4 feet below ground, level the ground for 4 feet on all sides, with a slight slope away from the spa to permit runoff.

STEP 2
EXCAVATING THE HOLE

With a shovel, dig a rough hole to accommodate your spa. Overcut the hole so that it is 6 inches larger on horizontal spa surfaces and 10 inches larger on vertical surfaces to allow room for plumbing and for sand backfill. Be sure the dirt on the bottom is firm and solidly packed. If the drain is in the bottom of the spa, cut a trench across the bottom of the hole large enough for the drainpipe. The rim of the spa should be slightly higher than the patio surface to keep dirt and rainwater from running in, so add the thickness of the patio brick or masonry to your measurement of the hole depth.

STEP 3
DIGGING THE PLUMBING TRENCH

After you've dug the hole for the spa shell and packed the bottom, excavate the trench between the spa shell and its support equipment. From the side of the spa where the plumbing stubs connect, dig a straight trench 10 to 12 inches wide to where the support equipment will be located. All plumbing runs in one trench for most installations. If you want to have underwater lights in your spa, you will need to run electrical lines from the spa shell in a *separate* trench.

PREPARING THE SPA SITE

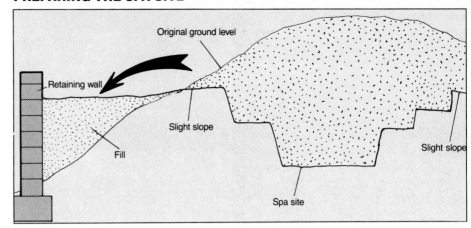

1. If the ground is level, you won't need to grade it. If the site is sloping, level it by taking dirt from high spots and filling in the low ones. Have the ground slope slightly down for about a yard all around the spa to allow water runoff, especially for in-ground spas.

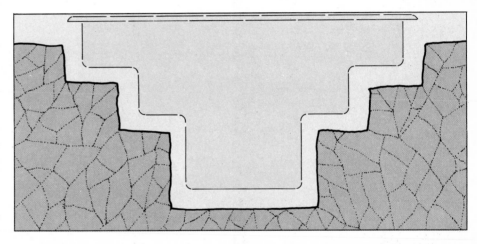

2. In-ground spas require no foundation. But dig the excavation larger than the spa to allow room for a sand backfill. The hole must also be large enough to accommodate the plumbing. Overdigging or underdigging may cause trouble in seating the spa.

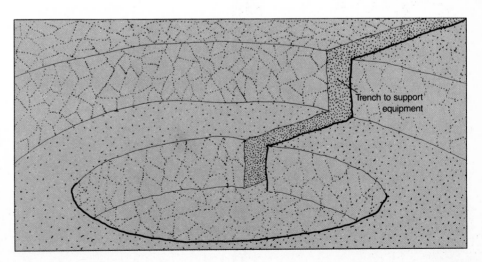

3. One trench accommodates all the plumbing for water circulation through the support system. Place it in direct line to the support system location. Dig other trenches for electricity for underwater lights or for a water faucet.

STEP 4
DIGGING THE UTILITIES TRENCH

The next step is to dig a straight trench from the support equipment area to the gas and electrical utilities outlets on your property. The most commonly used pipes are made of PVC—flexible polyvinyl chloride. They should lie about 18 inches below the ground; however, if the ground surface is covered with a wood deck or a masonry floor, PVC pipes need to be only about 12 inches below the ground. Metal pipes are more cumbersome but less expensive than PVC pipes, and many spa installers choose them instead. Metal pipes should be at least 12 inches below the ground, regardless of what is on the surface.

STEP 5
USING PVC PIPES

A special PVC pipe marked "natural gas" is used for the gas line; it must be installed so that an inspector can easily see the wording. Cut the pipe with a hacksaw and remove all burrs with a sharp knife. Roughen all pipe ends with medium-grit sandpaper to create a better bond. Trial-fit all pieces before gluing. Coat all ends with a primer; then apply a light coat of glue to the fitting and a heavy coat to the pipes. On unthreaded pipes, turn the pipe about a quarter turn to spread out the glue, then realign it, holding it for 60 seconds until the glue dries.

STEP 6
INSTALLING JET PLUMBING

Connect the jets to the water manifold and connect the manifold to the hot-water outlet pipe with a T-fitting. You can run flexible PVC pipe to the heater outlet once the spa is set in the ground. You must run rigid PVC pipe from the T-joint to a point on the spa near the trench before the spa is set. On two-pump systems, run the manifold line to the pump that controls hydrojets. Connect air lines either from the jets to the individual control dials on the lip of spa or into a common air line that leads to a

PREPARING THE SPA SITE (CONTINUED)

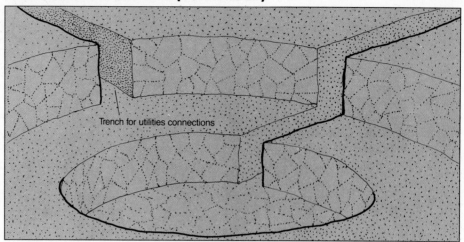

4. A second major trench from the support system to the utility hook-ups needs to be deep enough to provide security for the pipes. PVC pipes generally must be buried deeper than metal pipes, unless the surface level is concrete.

WORKING WITH PVC PIPE

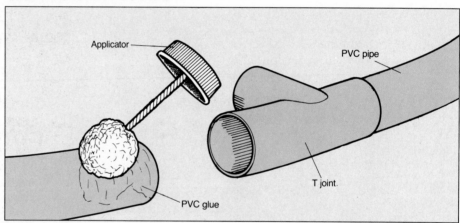

Coat PVC pipes with primer an inch beyond the connection so a building inspector can verify that it has been properly sealed. PVC pipe requires special glue that dries very quickly, so be prepared to work fast.

SPA PLUMBING COMPONENTS

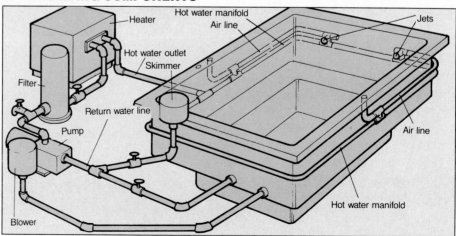

This illustration shows a typical spa plumbing scheme. Most spas can be installed with flexible PVC piping. Water lines are usually 1½ inches in diameter. Air lines can be from ½ inch to 1½ inches depending on the type of jet.

single control valve. You don't need to run air and water manifolds all the way around the spa. Instead, run them to the T-fittings located midway between jets; for example, if the spa has six jets, locate the T-joint between the third and fourth jets.

STEP 7
CONNECTING THE DRAINS AND SKIMMER

You may need two drains to satisfy local codes: a second drain located on the side of the spa reduces suction force in the main drain. The two drains should be 12 inches apart. Connect both drains and the skimmer to a common pipe with 1½-inch PVC. Both the drain lines and the skimmer line end in a T-joint that faces the direction of the trench when the spa is in the ground. Connect this assemblage to the suction line leading to the pump.

STEP 8
INSTALLING THE AIR BLOWER

Connect a 2-inch flexible PVC pipe from the air-channel inlet in the spa to the trench that leads to the air blower. If the distance from spa to air blower is more than 20 feet, make a loop in the air line by running PVC pipe from the air channel up to the lip of the spa, then back down to trench level and on to the blower. The loop prevents water from getting into the line between the spa and the blower. Too much water in the air line strains the blower when it pushes it back into the spa. It also causes a lag period between the time the blower is turned on and the first air enters the spa. In cold climates the loop prevents water from freezing and bursting the air line.

STEP 9
TESTING FOR LEAKS

After the pipes for the jets, drains, and skimmer are cut to fit, glued, and dried, set the spa on 2 × 4s on blocks to support it above ground, away from all excavations. Either close off the pipe ends with specially made testing plugs or run lengths of flexible PVC pipe up to

SPA DRAIN REQUIREMENTS

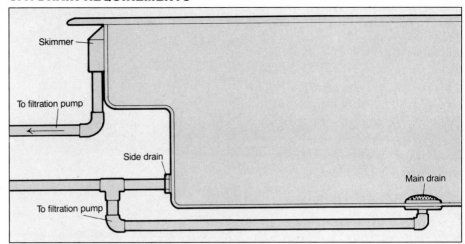

The forceful suction in some bottom drains poses a safety problem for people with long hair. Local safety codes may require a second drain located on the side of the spa and at least 12 inches from the bottom drain to reduce the pull.

INSTALLING THE BLOWER

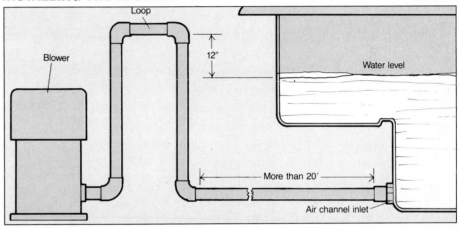

Install the air blower according to the manufacturer's instructions, mounting it 12 inches above the water level of the spa. If this is not possible, make a loop in the air line that rises 12 inches above the water level as shown.

TESTING PLUMBING INSTALLATION

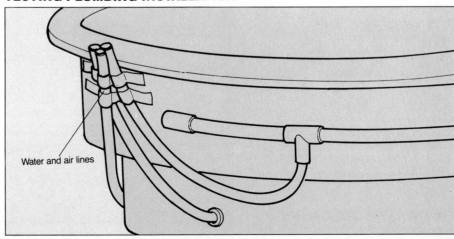

Before setting the spa in the excavation, test the plumbing for leaks. Wait at least 1 hour for the glue to dry and then fill the spa with water. Tape all the lines together, as shown. If there are no leaks, drain the spa, tipping it to remove all water.

a position above water level and tape them to the lip of the spa. Fill the spa with water to a point just below the skimmer trap. Wait one hour. Then check all plumbing joints and the air-channel inlet on the spa. If the air channel leaks, call the dealer for instructions on what to do about it. If there are no leaks, remove the tape and drop the pipes below water level or remove the testing plugs. Drain the water.

STEP 10
SETTING THE SPA

Cover the bottom of the hole with a layer of sand, 4 to 5 inches for a spa with a bottom drain, 2 to 3 inches for a side drain. Avoid scratching the interior of the spa: never stand or lay tools in it. With two assistants, carefully set the spa into the excavation with the plumbing stubs positioned at the head of the trench. Make sure the top lip of the spa sits slightly above the patio surface. Adjust this level by either adding more sand or digging the hole deeper. Using a 2 × 4 and a carpenter's level, position the spa so it is level *in all directions*.

STEP 11
PLACING THE PRELIMINARY BACKFILL

When the spa is positioned correctly, fill it with water to seat level and begin to backfill the excavation by pouring sand into the hole around the spa. Go slowly, adding several shovels of sand and wetting it with a garden hose so the sand packs lightly into the pockets around the sides and under the contours of the spa. Do not use too much water or the spa will float out of its bed. Check frequently with a level to make sure the spa is still well positioned. When the excavation is backfilled to seat level, stop and proceed to set up the support equipment.

STEP 12
CONNECTING THE SUPPORT EQUIPMENT TO THE SPA

For one-pump systems, connect the suction line to the pump inlet, then the pump inlet to the filter inlet. From there

PLACING THE SPA IN THE EXCAVATION

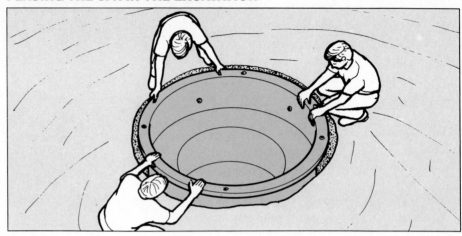

1. Spread a layer of sand on the bottom of the excavation. Then set the plumbed spa in the excavation with the help of two assistants to keep from dropping or scraping it. Never lift the spa by the plumbing connections or the fittings.

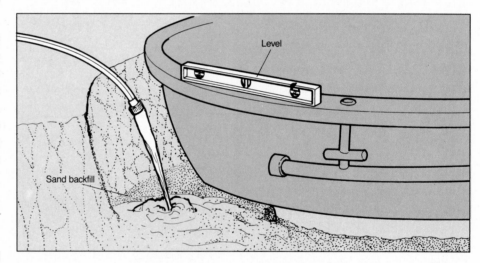

2. Be sure the spa is level; rock it back and forth if necessary. Then fill the spa with water, and backfill the excavation with sand. If the spa moves out of level, pour sand under the low points, wetting it so it flows under the foot-well of the spa. Make sure the sand packs tightly.

SPA WATER CIRCULATION

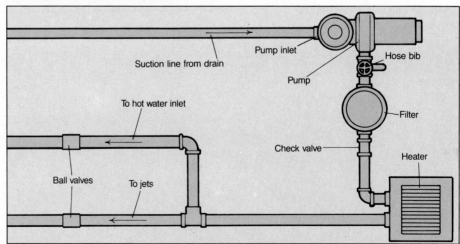

This diagram shows the flow of water through a typical support system. Dirty water is sucked out the drain by the pump; from there it passes through the filter and on to the heater. Warm water returns to the spa through the inlet pipes.

the line runs to the cold water inlet on the heater. For gas heaters, a check valve between the filter and the heater prevents hot water from siphoning back into the filter and ruining it. Last, run a line from the hot water outlet in the heater, back to the spa, connecting it to the jet manifold T, the hot water inlet, or both. On two-pump systems, the blower pump is connected to the jet manifold directly, bypassing the circulating pump-filter-heater system.

STEP 13
MOUNTING THE SUPPORT EQUIPMENT

Mount support equipment on concrete foundations. Follow your dealer's instructions for mounting skid packs. Align separate components so they can be connected together easily and are close to both trenches. Use flexible PVC pipe for all plumbing except the gas heater, where 2 to 3 feet of metal pipe must be run from the heater outlet to dissipate heat. (Check your local code.) Install a hose-bib fixture in the line between the pump and the filter to drain the spa. Lines running from the support equipment back to the spa must be the same diameter as the pipes used in preplumbing the spa and assembling the support equipment in order to prevent back pressure in the system.

STEP 14
MAKING THE UTILITY HOOK-UPS

The gas heater and the electrical lines run from the support equipment along a single trench and branch off to the gas meter and main electrical panel respectively. A licensed electrician should perform all wiring and hook-ups. Local building codes will determine the type of gas line needed. The vertical risers that enter and leave the trench must be made of steel. A 16-gauge metal tracer wire must run along the gas line so it can be located with a metal detector. A gas inspector will test your lines to make sure they can hold the required pressure.

COMPONENT ALIGNMENT

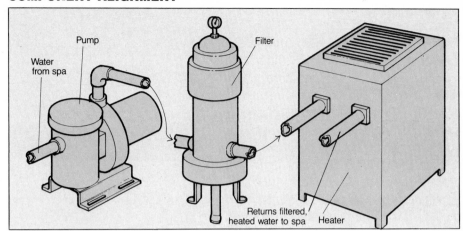

If you are installing individual components instead of a skid pack, be sure to connect them in proper order, as shown above. The flow of water is from the spa to the pump, through the filter to the heater, and finally, back to the spa.

ELECTRICAL HOOK-UP

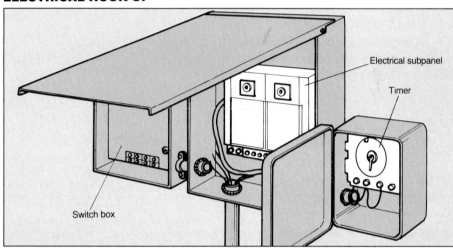

It is strongly recommended that you have a licensed electrician perform the final hook-up at the electrical panel. If your main service panel has no room for additional circuit breakers, have a subpanel installed.

GAS HOOK-UP

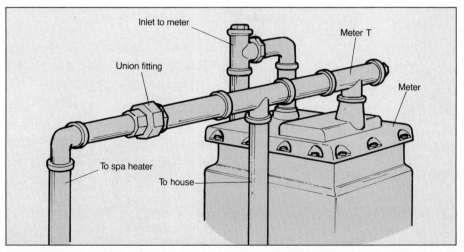

Connect the spa heater gas line to your gas meter with a union fitting, so that you can disconnect the spa gas supply without affecting the house gas. Check local building codes for approved gas hook-up requirements. It's usually easier and cheaper to use metal pipe.

STEP 15
COMPLETING THE INSTALLATION

After your equipment passes all the utility tests, clean the inside of the spa and fill it with water to just above the skimmer level. All the pipes should have water in them. Then tape plastic sheeting over the spa to keep sand out during the final backfilling. Follow the manufacturer's instructions for turning on the equipment. Make sure the pump is primed with water before turning it on. See that all equipment functions properly. If in doubt, turn everything off and call the dealer.

STEP 16
PLACING THE FINAL BACKFILL AND GRADING

If there are no leaks in the shell, complete the backfilling of the excavation and fill in the trenches. When you are backfilling the spa, continually check to make sure the spa shell is level and at its proper height. Also test the sand repeatedly to make sure that it is tightly packed. Set the final grading around the spa so that there is a slight and continual slope *away* from the spa for a distance of at least 10 feet. See Chapter 4, page 145, for testing and chemically balancing water.

COMPLETING THE PROJECT

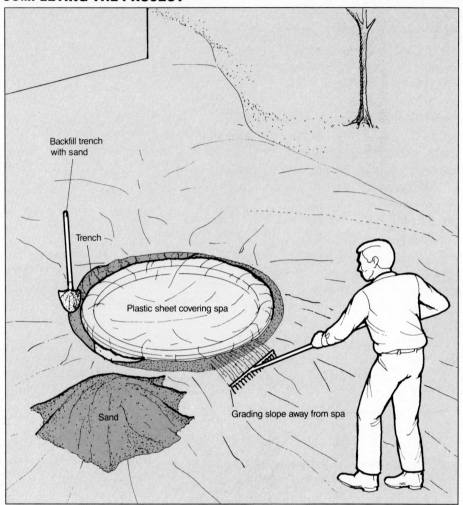

After the final backfill is completed, grade the area around the spa so that there is a gentle slope away from the lip. This will keep rainwater from washing dirt and debris into the bathing waters. Before using the spa, test and chemically treat the water.

COMPLETED OUTDOOR SPA PROJECT

As the focal point of an elevated deck, this spacious, blue-tiled spa offers relaxing space for as many as a dozen tired bathers.

This compact spa and its support equipment are installed completely above ground in a stepped, redwood enclosure.

Spa construction techniques permit virtually any shape, from free-form to the classic symmetry of this multi-curved design.

The bold, simple curve of this outdoor staircase encloses a cozy spa. The open railing opens up a view of the lake.

Even the simplest installation creates an attractive corner when set apart by protective shrubs and enlivened by brightly colored potted plants.

A backyard framed by tall trees on all sides incorporates a dramatic three-level deck, with a spa sitting at sunny mid-level.

A view from the base of the three-level deck (above) leads from the ground-level pool, up past the spa, to an outdoor eating area on the upper deck.

Warm-toned bricks attract sunlight and focus attention on this small spa, set among deep, tropical foliage at the edge of a dark redwood deck.

Placing this two-level deck directly beyond the double glass doors effectively extends the family recreation room into the backyard. Bathers can lounge in the sunny area of the spa and benches, or opt for the cool shade of the upper deck.

A sunken spa is the focal point in a broad deck that extends the entire width of the house; solarium windows join indoors and out.

A quiet grove of saplings surrounds this warm, russet-colored spa; the afternoon sun dapples broad surrounding benches with an invitation to relax.

Boulders and ferns turn a free-form tiled spa into a wild forest pool, set into the corner of a solarium.

The free-flowing curves of this black gunite (concrete) spa, nestled among evergreens, rocks, and waterfalls, create a peaceful setting.

A clever combination of real boulders set in gray gunite (concrete) results in a lush, enticing pool in this backyard corner.

Bathers in this free-form tiled spa can appreciate directly the exhilarating plunge of the adjacent waterfall.

The perfect symmetry of this combination spa and wading pool enhances the classic simplicity that characterizes an elegant patio and garden.

Flagstones of random shapes and sizes create rings that echo the outline of this free-form spa. Soon flowers will brighten the earth-filled niches that stretch out from both sides of a scaled-down waterfall.

The textural play of surfaces at work in this free-form spa installation sets dazzling geometric blue tiles against flat, many-sided flagstones, a rough stone wall, and well-tended gardens.

The dry, desert ambience of this backyard is enlivened by the spa, which offers the stimulation of bubbling water, and a gazebo providing cool shade.

The strong geometric pattern of the square and rectangular tiles of this backyard spa is repeated in surrounding stepped garden, fence, and high hedges.

Rough-hewn flagstone and low, sparse shrubbery create a rugged setting for this hexagonal spa.

A hot tub, sheltered in the crook of a stone wall, overlooks the calm waters of a pool; both are backed by a gently sloping rock garden.

Brilliant ultramarine tiles and a glistening sheet of waterfall make this circular spa a stunning visual and aural focal point.

This spa stands open to breezes and vistas on all sides, while the arbor above offers patches of shifting shade.

Water flows into this seven-sided spa from a sun-drenched rock garden above; a pool sits just on the other side of the spa.

A simple, square spa becomes a deep aquamarine jewel in this stark setting framed by massive walls and columns.

Long, low levels of tile and concrete lead gently to this deep, dark blue spa.

A royal blue spa is at the center of a stunning still life of large, white boulders, bright yellow and red dots of flowers, and strong vertical lines of green ferns.

China-blue tiled ledges and steps offer the bather a choice of levels on which to enjoy this spa—from toe dipping to total immersion.

A deep spa with an attenuated waterfall commands a sweeping view from the far end of this narrow condominium lot.

A bubbling spa, a covered hot tub, and a cool, calm pool—all integrated into one compact installation—fill the corner of this brick patio.

This foaming, angular spa, fed by a red- and black-tiled waterfall, is a stunning alternative to what would otherwise be an awkward corner.

In this unusual installation, an elevated spa overflows from two tiled waterfalls directly into the dark pool below.

This crimson-tiled octagonal spa is set in a broad wood deck and garden, overlooking an expansive recreation area.

Spa and pool are dramatically juxtaposed in this backyard: a dark wood deck frames the former, sweeping curves of white concrete enclose the latter.

Broad flagstones lend an outdoor feeling as they surround and support this large indoor spa; a wide mirror reflects natural light.

An octagonal corner spa is one of many comfortable appointments in this all-weather relaxing room; ceramic tiling makes maintenance easy.

A double spa, housed in a greenhouse attached directly to the main dwelling, offers year-round relaxation with an outdoor ambience. The small spa provides warmer water and more concentrated aeration, if desired.

This spa-solarium offers total climate control, with baseboard heating, air-conditioning, and thin venetian blinds to adjust sun, heat, and light.

Rich green foliage, indoors and out, and dark brown wood give this deep spa installation a feeling of quiet luxury that is enhanced by plush wall-to-wall carpeting.

One small, sunny corner of a recreation room is transformed by the gently swirling, inviting spa set on a low platform.

Installed without any excavation below grade, this bright spa beckons from a corner of a large bathing and exercise room.

Dominating this long solarium, a wide floor-level spa overflows directly into a slightly larger swimming pool.

Wood louvers create a quiet, private, but nonetheless breezy setting for this simple hot tub installation.

A broad avenue of weathered redwood planks leads to this circular hot tub, framed by latticework that recalls oriental architecture.

Constructed on a steep incline, this hot tub is surrounded by stairs that descend to the backyard pool area.

Viewed from above, this hot tub (below), mounted in a set of steep stairs between the upper deck and the recreation area in the lower backyard, seems to extend into space.

What at first glance appears to be a wishing well is actually a compact hot tub with its support equipment housed under a steeply gabled roof.

Twin, small-size hot tubs, installed on a raised deck, offer bathers the advantage of companionship as well as a choice of two water temperature levels.

This unobtrusive hot tub sits quietly in a well-lit corner of the enclosed part of a large patio; glass doors lead to the sunny deck outside.

Secure on its high deck aerie, this hot tub takes in the full view over a wild, boulder-strewn ravine leading down toward the sea.

Since this house sits on a hillside, a tiered recreational area was created by hanging a hot tub and deck in a corner, with stairs leading to the pool below.

This hot tub installation is kept private and cozy by a slatted surrounding fence, tall enough to ensure privacy.

A hot tub occupies the mid-point of an extensive deck that turns a steep backyard into a multi-level recreation spot.

By projecting out into lush, green woods, a spa takes full advantage of rustic surroundings.

2 SAUNAS

More than two thousand years ago, the Finns developed the custom of dry-heat bathing known as the sauna. Even today in Finland, the weekly sauna continues to be an eagerly awaited activity whether it be a family sauna, a get-together of special friends, or a solitary hour or two devoted to sweating and meditation. Indeed, traditional Finns consider time spent in the dry-heated room to be as sacred as the hours spent in church. In ancient times, the experience was steeped in ritual, honoring the elements of stone, fire, air, and water, all of which were viewed as gifts from the gods. Fire was especially appreciated in the wintry climate of the north, with its long, severe winters and cold, damp weather through much of the year. An old folk saying implies that the typical Finn will build and complete his sauna before he even begins to construct his home. And well he might, since the complete sauna can include most of the comforts of home and is far simpler and quicker to build.

The sauna is a type of bath in which the water used for cleansing is produced within the body, for it is really "perspiration bathing," a deep cleansing of the skin by flushing out impurities through the perspiring pores. In a small room heated to 190 or 200 degrees Fahrenheit (about 93 degrees Celsius) and with humidity below the 30 percent range, the body opens its pores and spontaneously and naturally begins to detoxify itself.

The complete sauna consists of alternating bouts of heat and cold. A bather spends 10 to 15 minutes in the heated stoveroom (or longer for seasoned sauna-takers) and follows it with a plunge into cold water. Customs vary, but an outdoor sauna usually includes a large tank or a pool nearby. For indoors, a shower or bathtub is used. Of course, if you're lucky enough to have a lake or river handy, a quick swim is a most natural and refreshing way to cool off. In winter the very hearty may enjoy a roll in the snow.

A sauna may last anywhere from one to three hours, alternating sessions of heat and cold, and including a final washing up and time to relax in the after-sauna room, which is designed as a restful refuge where one allows the body temperature to return slowly to normal. Many sauna enthusiasts include a brief nap or a cup of hot tea or coffee as part of the post-sauna ritual. If time permits, this relaxed period alone can be the perfect antidote to the stress and demands of the world outside the sauna.

The stoveroom is truly an escape from the external world—a quiet room with subdued lighting—and paneled with soft, comforting wood. The extreme heat is produced by about 70 pounds of igneous rocks warmed by a

A BASEMENT SAUNA COMPLEX

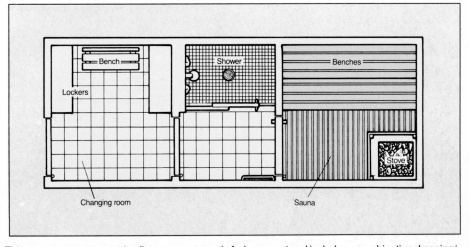

This compact sauna complex fits across one end of a basement and includes a combination dressing/relaxation room, a shower, and a stoveroom.

small stove fueled by wood, gas, or electricity. Traditionally, saunas built outdoors were heated by wood-burning stoves; but with more saunas being built in modern homes and apartments, electricity has replaced the stacks of wood. But whatever the fuel used, the soft, gentle heat radiated by stones can be withstood longer than the strident heat generated directly from fuel.

Occasionally bathers will ladle a splash of water from a wooden bucket onto the rocks to produce a burst of steam, what Native Americans in their own sweat lodges called "Grandfather's breath." The splash of steam adds moisture to the room and prevents the body from becoming too dehydrated. To stimulate circulation, bathers whisk their bodies with bundles of leafy birch twigs or pine boughs called vihtas. Not only does the light slap on the skin refresh the mind and body, but also the sweet scent of birch or pine aromatizes the room. Whisking one another's bodies in a communal sauna is an expression of friendship and harmony.

The beneficial effects of the sauna include cleansing the complexion, relaxing and reviving muscles after vigorous workouts, stimulating circulation, enhancing mental alertness, sharpening the senses, and even relieving the symptoms of minor colds and illnesses.

If you're healthy enough to participate in most amateur sports, you're probably healthy enough to take a sauna. But health authorities suggest that people with heart problems, diabetes, high blood pressure, and those who are on medication such as tranquilizers, antihistamines, or antibiotics should consult their physicians before taking a sauna. Whatever your state of health, the sauna should not be misused by overindulgence. The Finns traditionally took only one sauna a week and found that sufficient. Modern people tend to overdo most good things. Excessive bathing in a sauna is not recommended.

Saunas are wonderfully adaptable enclosures that can be built in the smallest of closets or constructed as complete cottages out in the woods. They can be built as self-contained structures or as simple rooms in a larger building. Only basic carpentry skills are needed to build one to your own specifications.

In recent years sauna dealers have built or imported Finnish saunas as prefabricated kits. These complete sauna rooms come shipped in knocked-down modular units with easy-to-read instructions. All the necessary hardware is furnished in the package, which makes it easy for any do-it-yourselfer to construct his or her own sauna in a matter of hours. The prefab saunas require no studding or dropped ceiling. They can stand virtually anywhere without requiring any major alterations to the surrounding area.

BASIC SAUNA COMPONENTS

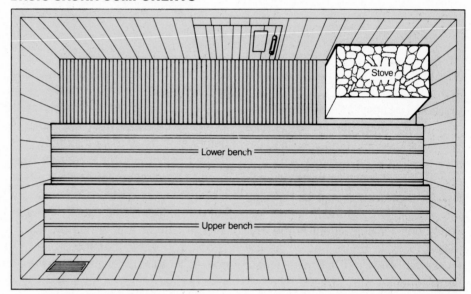

This bird's-eye view shows how the stoveroom makes a wood-paneled environment around a confined stove, benches, and duckboards.

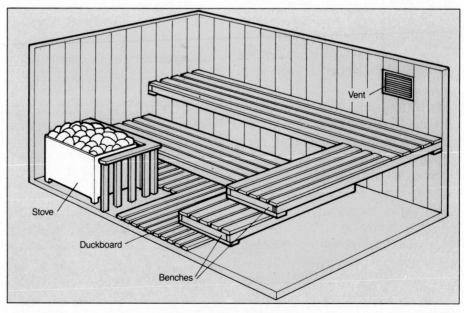

This cutaway view shows two levels of benches, with a warmer spot near the ceiling, and a cooler area on the lower level.

Sauna Stoverooms

The stoveroom is the heart of the sauna complex; in fact, when most people use the term *sauna*, they are referring to the stoveroom alone. In essence, the stoveroom is a tightly insulated, wood-lined room with a very simple, restful, and efficient design. The typical sauna is square or rectangular in shape and contains a stove (with guardrail), two or three tiers of benches, duckboard flooring, and vents.

The proportions of the stoveroom are critical to the sauna's performance. If you want the proper marriage of heat and comfort, you need to strike a careful balance between the total area available for the sauna, the number of bathers you wish to accommodate at one time, the size of the stove, the amount and arrangement of bench space, the thickness of the insulation, and the size and positioning of the vents.

STOVEROOM SIZES

An efficient and enjoyable stoveroom can be designed to accommodate anywhere from one or two people to a dozen or more. A small stoveroom might be as compact as 3 × 3 feet wide and 7 feet high, which could fit easily into a bedroom closet or a corner of the basement or attic. A stoveroom that is 10 feet by 14 feet wide by 7 feet high is a good-sized room, found in free-standing saunas that are miniature cottages in themselves and are most often built apart from the home. A popular size for family use is 8 feet by 10 feet by 7 feet high. This stoveroom size can seat four or five people comfortably and can still be incorporated inside the house. It doesn't require the stove capacity that larger rooms do, and it can also be built with less lumber and materials.

In theory a stoveroom should provide at least 65 cubic feet per bather. This allows each bather sufficient stretching and breathing room—an important consideration in an environment that is relatively small and well insulated—and helps to guarantee a constant inside temperature. The ceiling of the stoveroom should never be more than 7 feet high. A low ceiling design keeps heat down close to the bathers and prevents the slight drafting that can occur when there is more space for air to circulate upward. Some saunas slant the ceiling from about 5 feet high at the wall where the stove is located to 7 feet high at the back walls, where tiered benches enable bathers to enjoy the hottest area in the room.

A guiding principle for designing a stoveroom is to offer the maximum amount of seating and reclining space per bather, given the total dimensions of the stoveroom perimeter. Interior floor space can be reduced to a minimum since walking around is not a sauna activity. Bench arrangements

BASIC SAUNA LAYOUTS

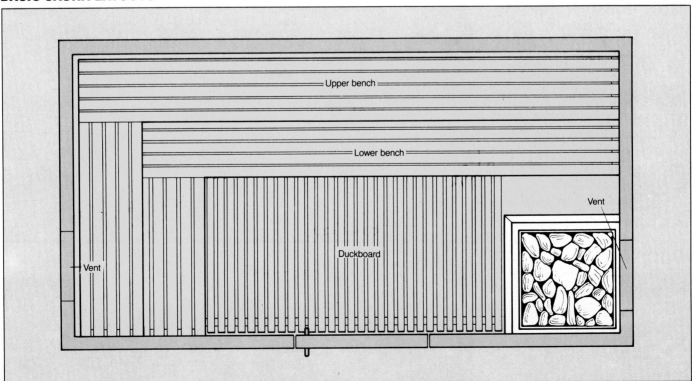

The simplest sauna layout, perfect for small areas, is a straight-line design with the benches along one wall.

can follow an L-shaped or a U-shaped plan or a simpler plan featuring along one wall a straight bench that is tiered in two or three levels to allow areas of greater or lesser heat intensity. Benches should be about 1½ to 2 feet wide so that bathers can be comfortable reclining as well as sitting. A good rule of thumb for bench length is to figure about 24 inches for each seated bather.

DOORS AND SIDINGS

The sauna door offers the major spot for potential heat leakage from a stoveroom. For this reason, it is tight fitting, heavily insulated, and small in size. This helps reduce the loss of interior heat through the seams between the door and the wall as well as through the open door when bathers come and go between sessions. The door always swings outward for the convenience of the bather who is leaving the stoveroom as well as for the comfort and safety of bathers who are still inside. The door never has any lock or latch that might trap someone inside.

Many people prefer a small window in their sauna to provide a modicum of light and perhaps a pleasant view. A window also prevents the claustrophobic sensations or feelings of tedium that a small room may produce. Of course, there's nothing preventing a sauna from having a large window, a skylight for seeing stars at night, or even an entire glass wall, except that glass is not as good an insulator as wood. Sauna designers recommend a window size equal to at least 5 percent of the floor area.

Every sauna needs fresh air. A complete and effective ventilation system consists of a fresh-air intake behind the stove near the floor and an exhaust flue located on the opposite wall near the ceiling. A few inches cut off the bottom of the door can also serve as the intake vent.

The overwhelming majority of stoverooms are either square or rectangular, but there are exceptions. In addition to rooms with sloped ceilings rising from

BASIC SAUNA LAYOUTS (CONTINUED)

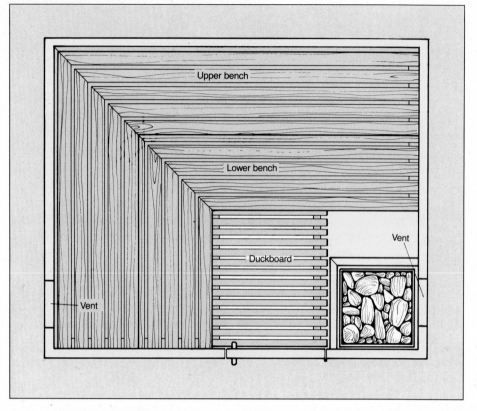

For larger spaces, an L-shaped stoveroom not only allows more bench room, but lets bathers get farther away from the stove.

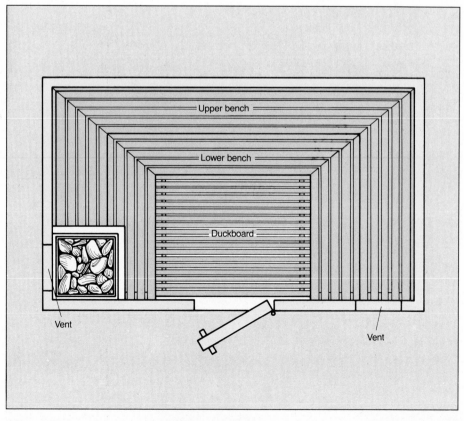

A large U-shaped sauna accommodates many bathers and has a "hot spot" immediately next to the stove.

the wall behind the stove to the wall behind the highest tier, as mentioned above, there are round, trapezoidal, domed, and teepee-style stoverooms. Most homeowners, however, find that the simple square or rectangular shapes are the most practical. A unique model shaped like a large barrel is also on the market.

The interior of the stoveroom is usually wood, although other materials such as tile and masonry are used. The reason wood is still preferred after so many years of experimentation is that it is a comforting texture that is not too hot to touch even when heated. Of course, if your sauna is built outdoors you can use a natural rock wall for one side or a corner of your stoveroom, and build a sauna around it.

The wood for the interior walls should be soft, low density, and heat resistant. Redwood, cedar, and pine are best. The wood should be free of knotholes and sap pockets that could drip when hot. Simple panels of tongue-and-groove construction make a solid interior that is both attractive and well insulated.

CONSTRUCTION TYPES

There are three basic modes of stoveroom construction: prefab, precut, and custom-built. Each format produces a strong, comfortable, efficient stoveroom. The format that is right for you depends on your budget, your time, your basic carpentry skills, and, most significantly, the design of the sauna you want.

The simplest stoveroom to install is, of course, the prefabricated, modular stoveroom built in the United States or imported from Finnish manufacturers and available through suppliers in this country. Some dealers even provide installation services; but the prefab sauna is easy to set up and ideal for homeowners who want to do their own work but who have limited carpentry skills and not much time to spare. A prefab stoveroom can be installed and ready to use in one day.

All the pieces in a prefab stoveroom

BARREL-SHAPED SAUNAS

Barrel-shaped stoveroom designs make great freestanding saunas either outdoors or indoors. The womblike interior of a barrel-shaped stoveroom is warm and comforting. It is also very fuel-efficient.

PREFAB SAUNA COMPONENTS

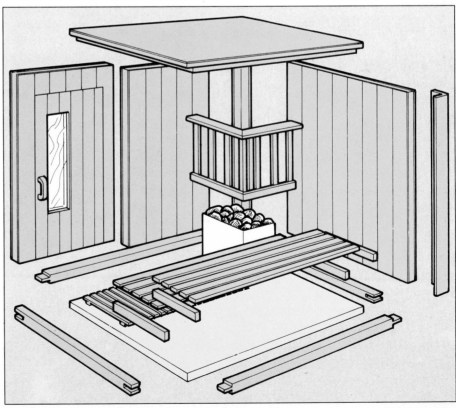

This exploded drawing of a prefab sauna shows the major components that come already assembled, including wall panels, door panel, benches, and ceiling.

kit snap and lock into place, including the floor, walls, ceiling, benches, door, and stove. Most kits use a simple, easy-to-follow numbering system for all parts. Some outdoor kits include exterior siding and roofing as well. A complete sauna package comes with additional rooms for dressing, relaxation, and even a shower stall.

The precut stoveroom is midway between the prefab and the custom-built types. It consists of walls, floors, and ceiling cut to your own specifications by a reliable sauna dealer. In effect you create your own unassembled sauna ready to take home and put together yourself.

The precut stoveroom is a good choice for homeowners who have basic carpentry skills and who enjoy do-it-yourself work. It's also an easy solution for homeowners who cannot find a prefab stoveroom to fit the shape or design they want. Precut stoverooms do not have the simple snap-together assembly mechanisms that prefab saunas have, but virtually any precut sauna stoveroom requires nothing more complicated than hammering nails.

A precut stoveroom can be either less or more expensive than a prefab stoveroom, based upon the design specifications you present to the sauna dealer.

A custom-built stoveroom is one that either you or professional sauna builders design and construct to meet the unique features of your site and to satisfy your personal desires in terms of size and accommodations.

The most expensive of all stoveroom construction modes, custom-building is also the most versatile. If, for example, you want to build a sauna with an unusual geometric floor plan, or a series of window views, or contoured benches, or special equipment for bathers with physical impairments, a custom-built sauna may be your only alternative. Some of the expense can be alleviated by contracting the more difficult jobs while doing the simpler jobs yourself.

PRECUT SAUNA ASSEMBLY

A precut sauna is delivered with all lumber cut to size, but completely unassembled. You assemble the wall frames and paneling, and set them up as shown above.

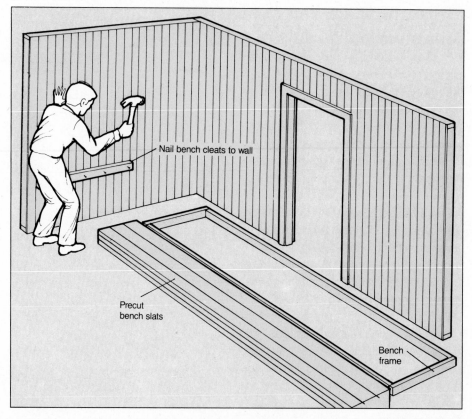

After you have assembled the walls and set them up, you can proceed to install the benches, floors, and finally, the ceiling.

Sauna Combinations

Some homeowners stop with the installation of a stoveroom; but to derive full benefit from sauna bathing, you need a complete sauna complex. This becomes especially important if you wish to provide family members and guests with a dependably comfortable experience each time the sauna is used. Part of that experience involves efficient pre-stoveroom preparation and post-stoveroom relaxation and cleansing. If you rely on standard bathroom, bedroom, or lounging facilities to answer these needs, you often lose that efficiency.

The complete sauna complex can consist of four or five rooms or sections of a room, depending on how extensive you intend to make your sauna program. Besides the stoveroom, which is the most significant but not always the

biggest component of the sauna, there can be a dressing area, a cold-water area (typically a shower), a relaxation room with kitchen facilities, and a supply room.

DRESSING ROOM

The dressing room is for bathers to change clothes. Since a sauna is most often taken in the nude, there should be hooks to hang clothes on, shelves on which to leave watches and jewelry, a place for shoes, and a supply of towels or robes for wearing around the sauna before going into the stoveroom. The dressing room is also a place to store bathing suits, wraps, or towels that may be worn inside the sauna. If the sauna is detached from the house, bathers arriving there in the winter may be wearing heavy, wet coats that re-

quire special hanging facilities.

A dressing room also provides a pleasing transitional area between the stoveroom and the rest of the house or property. Final decisions about the size and amenities of the dressing room depend upon how many people you plan to entertain in the sauna and whether they will be primarily family members (who may be content with a more primitive arrangement) or guests (whom you will want to entertain more formally).

COLD-WATER AREAS

Between sessions in the stoveroom, bathers emerge to cool off by plunging themselves into cold water. This plunge also exercises the pores, stimulates circulation, and helps to remove impurities from the body surface. The pre-

DRESSING ROOM COMPONENTS

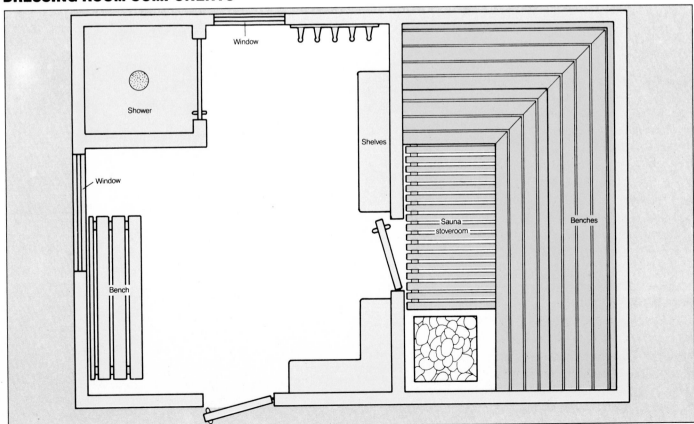

The dressing room is an integral part of a sauna. Here there are relaxation benches, pegs for clothes, and shelves for linens.

cise type of cold-water area you can have adjacent to your stoveroom varies greatly depending on whether your sauna complex is indoors or outdoors.

An outside tank or tub is ideal because it allows your bather to breathe clean fresh air. If you can locate your sauna near a swimming pool, you'll have the cold rinse problem taken care of, at least in good weather. Many homeowners with pools, however, prefer outdoor tank, tub, or shower cleansing (at least initially) to prevent post-stoveroom bathers from adding impurities to the pool water. This is a particular concern in the case of saunas that will service relatively large numbers of people.

Indoor saunas usually rely on an indoor shower stall located close to the stoveroom. Preferably it should be located right next to the wooden flooring of the sauna complex for the safety of the bathers and for easy maintenance. A shower of this type may also be used to clean the body before entering the sauna, which can add greatly to the bather's enjoyment.

A shower, tank, or tub requires good drainage, especially if it is a tank and hose arrangement where enthusiastic bathers will be inclined to dunk and splash each other with cold water.

RELAXATION ROOMS

An important phase of the sauna ritual is the relaxation period that follows bathing. One should not dress immediately and hurry back to the outside world. Even though a cold shower reinvigorates the skin, the body temperature needs to return to normal slowly and naturally. Otherwise the bather will continue to feel overheated and even light-headed for up to an hour after the sauna bath itself.

The most enjoyable and complete resting room accommodates sufficient cots, daybeds, or lounges for your average number of bathers. You may want to install a radio or tape deck to provide soft music, a small stovetop to prepare hot chocolate or a light snack, and a rack for books and magazines.

AN OUTDOOR SAUNA COMPLEX

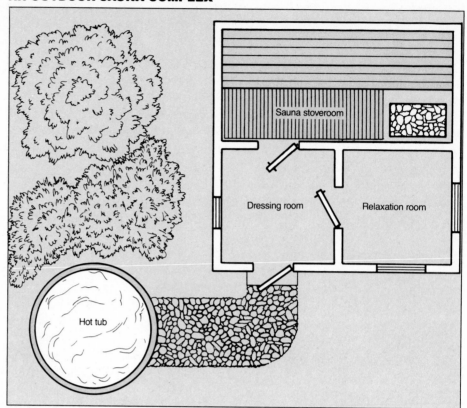

The ground around the tank area outside the sauna should be stone or wood chips to prevent mud being carried back inside.

RELAXATION ROOM AMENITIES

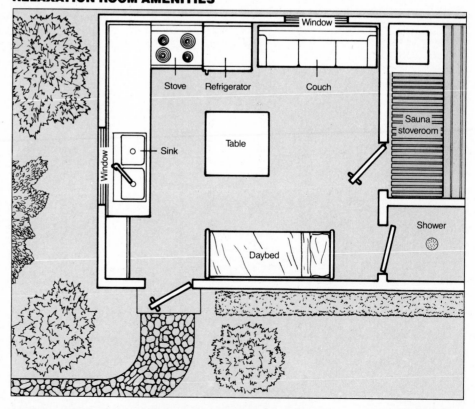

A full-sized relaxation room near the sauna can include kitchen facilities, a daybed, stereo, TV, and reading materials.

Ventilation, Insulation, and Wiring

A sauna complex is actually a very simple arrangement of basic parts, as befits the traditional sauna bathing ritual. There are, however, details aside from the structural components of the sauna complex and the stove itself that need to be considered. They relate to the ventilation, insulation, electrification, and lighting of the stoveroom.

VENTILATION

A stoveroom needs to have adequate ventilation for the comfort and health of the bathers, especially if it contains a gas or wood-burning stove. These fuels deplete the oxygen in the air and can cause bathers to become dizzy. Even with an electrical stove, the air in the sealed room can quickly become heavy with carbon dioxide from the bathers' lungs.

An air intake duct should be located near the floor on the wall by the stove (preferably behind the stove). An exhaust duct should be located on the wall opposite the intake duct, at a higher level. The precise arrangement to give your sauna the optimum air circulation depends on the specific design of your sauna. The placement and design of the benches as well as the proportions of the room itself all have an impact on how high the exhaust duct should be and whether it should be directly across from the intake duct.

An adjustable slide panel on the exhaust duct regulates the amount of air leaving the room and the flow rate of the ventilation. The exhaust duct could pass into the dressing or relaxation room to heat it. If the exhaust duct goes outside, install an up-draft duct to prevent backflow that would pull in colder outside air.

Consult with your municipal building department to find out what the local code requires in terms of sauna stoveroom ventilation. Usually a safe estimate is to provide an exhaust duct

SAUNA AIRFLOW

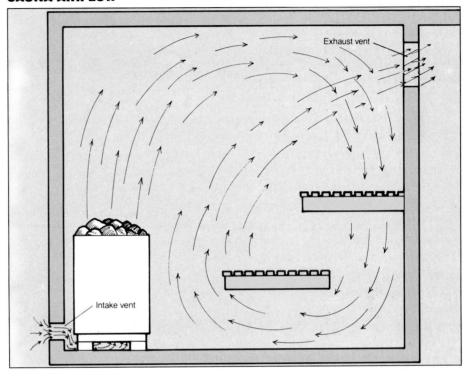

A sauna must have adequate ventilation for safety and health reasons. This airflow pattern is standard in most saunas.

INSULATING THE WALLS

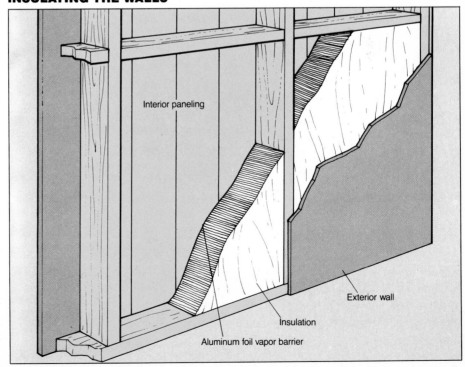

The best insulation materials include batts of fiberglass with one foil-covered side that faces into the stoveroom to reflect heat.

whose cross section equals 1/20 of the floor area, but never less than 1½ square feet.

INSULATION

The stoveroom must be well insulated to keep heat in and cold and dampness out. Good insulation also serves to block noises from the outside world. The easiest and most efficient way to accomplish these purposes is to use batts of fiberglass insulation stapled within the walls, inside the ceiling, and under the floor of the stoveroom.

The fiberglass batts should be installed so that they form air pockets within walls, floor, and ceiling. These pockets are themselves excellent insulators. Staple insulation batts with the foil face toward the interior of the sauna so that the foil faces into the room to create a vapor barrier and reflect heat back into the room.

ELECTRICITY

If any mistakes are made in the installation of electrical wires, the results can be disastrous. Hire a professional electrician to wire your stove, control panel, thermostat, and lighting.

The electrical wiring in a sauna stoveroom goes behind the insulation batts, where it will stay dry. All wiring must be heat resistant; and to avoid possible accidents, all switches must be installed on the outside of the stoveroom.

LIGHTING

Light passing through the window in the sauna door can illuminate the stoveroom sufficiently for sauna bathing purposes. Most people, however, like to create a special atmosphere inside the stoveroom to separate it from outside reality.

The typical sauna light shines from a single source, covered with frosted or tinted glass. If you wish to use a soft lamp inside your stoveroom, place it high on a wall as far away from the stove as possible. Vapor-sealed fixtures prevent moisture from collecting

in the light. The light switch must be installed outside the room. For a subdued or romantic touch, a simple candle or two in a metal dish that will collect the melted wax may be all the light you need.

INSULATING THE FLOOR

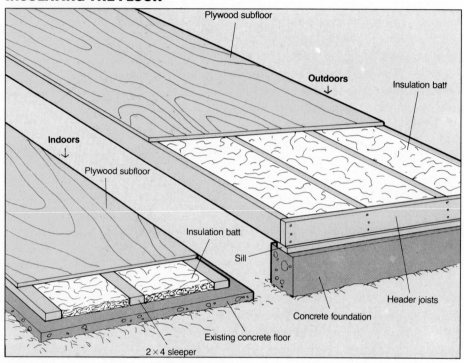

To insulate an indoor floor, lay 2 × 4 sleepers on the broad side, insulation batts between them, and cover with plywood subflooring. An outdoor floor will require 2 × 10 joists supported on a sill with insulating batts placed between them.

ELECTRICAL CONTROL CENTER

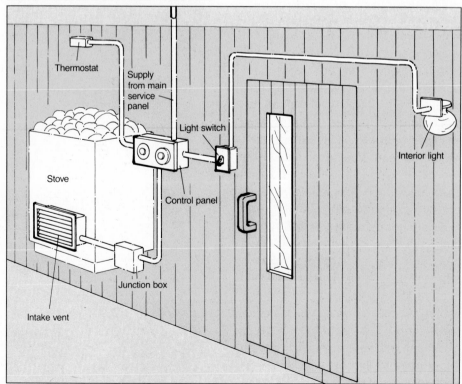

One control panel mounted outside on the sauna wall controls all the electrical fixtures inside the stoveroom.

Sauna Heating

Traditionally, sauna stoverooms were heated by wood-burning stoves, but the popularity of the home sauna in this century was triggered by the development of electrical and gas stoves. While the electrical stove is currently the most commonly used, each type continues to have its own particular advantages and disadvantages; you should test your wishes and needs against each type before making a final choice.

WOOD-BURNING STOVES

The original wood-burning stoveroom heaters consisted of a pile of stones placed on a rack above a brick or masonry fire box. Heat from the fire warmed the stones, and the stones, in turn, warmed the air. The mystique of wood-burning stoves still holds an allure for many sauna bathers, and the scent of aromatic wood burning nearby unquestionably adds to the enjoyment of sauna bathing.

Of course, there are some drawbacks to this traditional heating method. Burning wood produces soot and needs frequent stoking; and a stoveroom that burns wood will also require a flue and a chimney. All in all, there is more work involved with wood-burning stoves: collecting the wood, chopping it, and cleaning out the ashes. Furthermore, a wood-fueled stove does not warm up the room as fast as a gas or electric stove. A medium-sized stoveroom could take 3 to 4 hours to reach ideal bathing heat if heated by a wood-burning stove. Reasonable fireproofing (such as brick) must be installed around the stove, on the floor, and on the wall behind the stove. Like the other two models, the wood-burning stove must also be set well out from the wall.

If you're planning to build a sauna with a wood-burner, you need to decide how you want the fire to be fueled and stoked. If you want the bather to be able to fuel and stoke the stove from within the stoveroom, you need to provide space there for storing at least a small pile of wood and all necessary stoking implements. If you want to fuel and stoke the stove from outside the stoveroom, you need to build an extension that reaches from the stove itself into the next room where you can keep your supply of wood and tend the fire.

WOOD-BURNING STOVE DESIGN

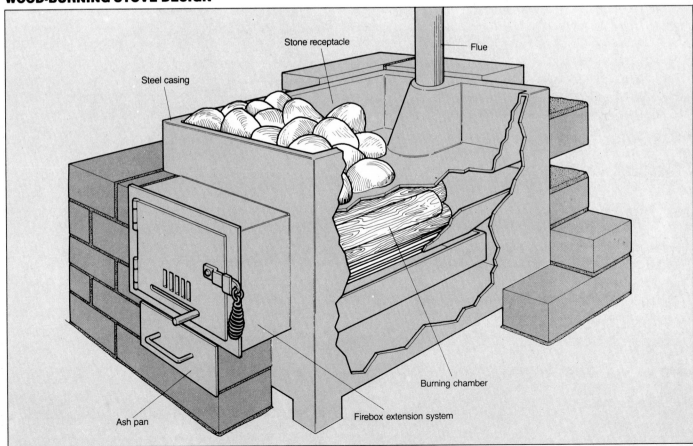

Modern wood-burning stoves come in different sizes and are as cleanly designed as the electric and gas versions.

Some companies sell prefabricated metal stoves with extensions for this purpose.

The best wood fuel for a sauna stoveroom is dense wood that burns slowly, produces an even heat, and doesn't generate a lot of soot. Birch, elm, and oak are favorite woods of this type, followed by ash, fir, and maple. You'll also want a wood that releases a pleasant scent (which all of the above woods do). Whichever wood you use, it should be well seasoned—at least 6 months.

GAS STOVES

Many homeowners prefer a gas stove in their sauna stoveroom because it is less expensive to operate than an electric one and easier to operate than a wood one. In terms of energy use, gas is far more fuel efficient than the alternatives.

In the gas stove, a constant flow of gas is released into a metal combustion chamber where it burns directly underneath a pile of stones. Fresh air is drawn in from outside the stoveroom, and fumes are discharged through an exhaust vent. A safety device attached to the stove automatically turns the gas flow off if the pilot light goes out.

A gas stove is far more convenient than a wood-burning stove, since its entire operation is thermostatically controlled. The popular size sauna stoveroom—5 feet by 7 feet by 7 feet high—requires a 16,000 BTU heater.

ELECTRIC STOVES

By far the most commonly used stove in home sauna complexes is the electric stove. Developed in the 1930s, it single-handedly revolutionized the use of saunas, primarily because the streamlined, compact stove unit can fit into the smallest apartment or closet area.

Electric sauna stoves are easy to install. They run clean and are inexpensive to operate in those areas where electricity is modestly priced. A 220-volt electrical system will handle the average-sized stove. A smaller electric

GAS-FUELED SAUNA STOVE

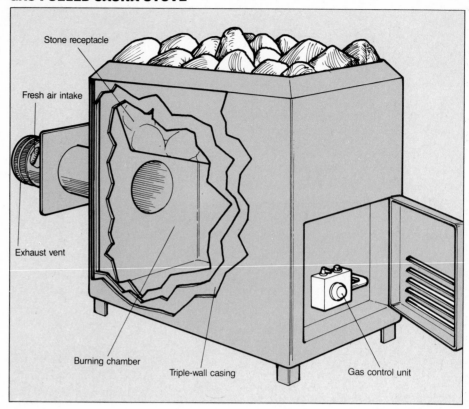

A gas-fueled stove requires a fresh-air intake and exhaust vent on the stove and a hook-up to the main gas line.

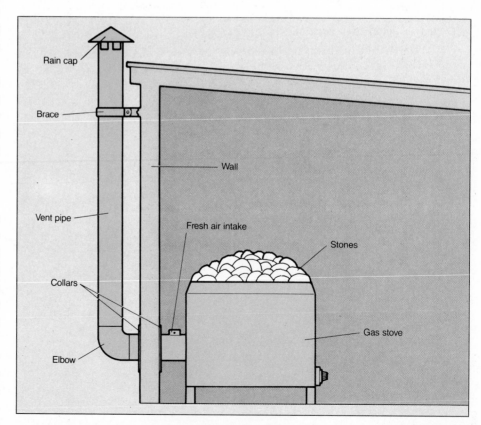

A gas-stove requires a flue vent to the outside of the stoveroom. Your stove supplier can furnish the necessary pipework, braces, wall collar, and vent cap to keep the rain out.

stove for a smaller sauna runs on 110-volt electrical supply.

The stones are either placed over the electric heating elements or distributed among them. The elements themselves are encased in several layers of noncorrosive metal. The outer sheath of the unit is made of stainless steel or a baked enamel to prevent heat loss and to keep the stove itself from becoming too hot, which would be dangerous for bathers.

Electric stoves are the least complicated in design. They require no special vents, flues, or chimneys and come in a wider variety of shapes than the other types of stoves. They can be free-standing or mounted on the wall to save floor space, which is at a premium in the extremely small saunas that the electric stove services so well. Their smallness and variety also permit more bench space and bench design options than wood-burning or gas stoves.

STOVE SIZE

The size of the sauna stove—wood-burning, gas, or electric—that is most appropriate for you depends on several factors, including the size of your stove-room and, if the sauna complex is located outside, the range of annual climates in your area. These same factors influence the choice of stove type that is most appropriate for you.

Gas sauna stoves have to produce 1,000 BTUs for every 15 cubic feet in the stoveroom; electric stoves consume 1 kilowatt for every 45 cubic feet. Electric stove models range from small units of 2.2 kilowatts to large ones of 18 kilowatts.

There is no easy formula for determining the best size for a wood-burning stove since the amount of heat that a wood-burning stove produces varies each session depending on the type and amount of wood used. A rough estimate is that a sauna big enough to service an average-sized family (four or five people) will consume about 44 pounds of dense wood (slightly over one cubic foot) in a single sauna bathing session.

ELECTRIC SAUNA STOVES

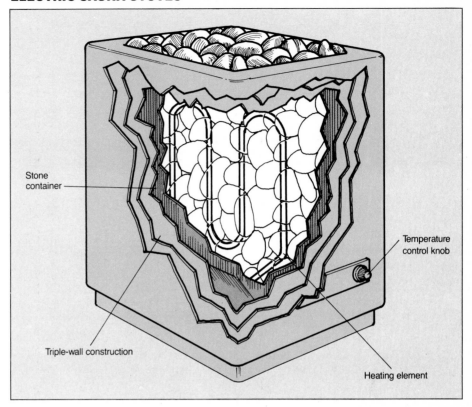

Stone container

Temperature control knob

Triple-wall construction

Heating element

The heating elements inside the wall of an electric stove loop up and down across the stone container.

SAUNA HEATING ALTERNATIVES

The most primitive-style saunas do not require hot rocks at all. Simply keep a wood fire burning in a conventional fireplace to heat a small, insulated room.

Sauna Accessories

A well-equipped sauna complex requires very little in the way of accessories. Headrests, backrests, and footrests are welcome additions to a flat bench; but other than the stove, the only mechanical devices you might want are a thermometer to measure room temperature and a hygrometer to read the humidity. For the most accurate readings, locate them about 6 feet from the ceiling, away from the stove, door, and ventilator. The humidity reading is important for saunas with electrically operated stoves, which tend to dry out the atmosphere more than gas- or wood-fueled stoves do. When the room gets too dry (you'll know when your nose gets irritated), splash water on the stones for more steam.

The wooden bucket and long-handled ladle are traditional pieces of equipment for the sauna, because, even though the sauna is known for its quiet, dry heat, sudden gusts of steam are important for the total therapeutic effect. Plastic buckets and ladles are available but should be kept far from the stove so that the heat won't damage them. Wooden ones, of course, take the heat better and complement the interior with a more natural look.

Vihtas are bunches of leafy branches, usually birch, pine, or eucalyptus twigs, that are used to strike the skin lightly during the sauna bath in order to stimulate circulation. When fresh and fragrant, they also aromatize the air, giving the room a pleasant outdoor scent. You can buy vihtas from sauna dealers or make your own. Ten to twenty twigs tied together make a nice bundle. Leaves should be dampened to release their fragrance.

The only other amenities you need are a good supply of clean towels, sponges, perhaps a loofah for removing dried skin, and several robes for wearing outside the stoveroom.

DESIGNS FOR COMFORT

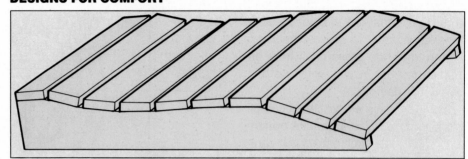

Headrests, backrests, and footrests are of similar construction, with rounded design to support parts of the body comfortably.

DEVICES FOR CONTROL

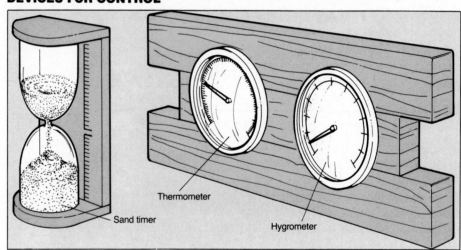

Sand timer

Thermometer

Hygrometer

Thermometers, hygrometers, and hourglasses monitor the environment and time the length of your stay in the sauna.

AIDS TO STIMULATION

A bucket of water and a ladle provide refreshing bursts of steam. A whisk of leafy sprigs, called a vihta, is used to strike the skin occasionally and stimulate circulation.

Selecting a Sauna

The first major decision a homeowner needs to make concerning a sauna installation is whether to locate the complex outdoors or indoors. If you have room, an outdoor sauna complex makes a real retreat from the stresses of everyday life. Unfortunately, it costs more to build an outdoor complex than an indoor one. An outdoor complex requires tighter insulation and, usually, higher heating costs since you'll have to heat the dressing room, the relaxation room, and perhaps a shower stall if the climate is so cold you cannot use an outdoor tank or shower. You may also have to run utility lines out to it. Don't overlook the added costs in constructing a concrete footing, exterior walls, and a roof. If there isn't any natural privacy, such as bushes provide, you may have to erect a fence or lattice.

The indoor sauna, of course, is unaffected by the weather and can be located near bathrooms and showers. Many are small enough to fit into unused corners of basements or attics, or large closets and pantries. They are always close to utility lines and often you can use an existing room, for post-sauna rest periods.

Before buying, research various manufacturers and models. Visit local dealers both to seek advice and to find out which ones are reputable and likely to be faithful suppliers. Check carefully the quality of the materials and the ease of installation. Be sure you know what the warranty covers.

There are many combinations of buying, hiring, and doing-it-yourself strategies for installing a sauna complex. You can save a lot of money if you're willing to do some of the construction work yourself and procure materials from hardware stores, lumber companies, and even neighborhood junk dealers.

BASIC OUTDOOR SAUNA STOVEROOM

This basic outdoor, freestanding sauna comes complete with all structural components, plus the minimum facilities of benches and stove. A wide variety of other models accommodate larger groups of bathers in more spacious designs.

INDOOR STOVEROOM COMPLEX

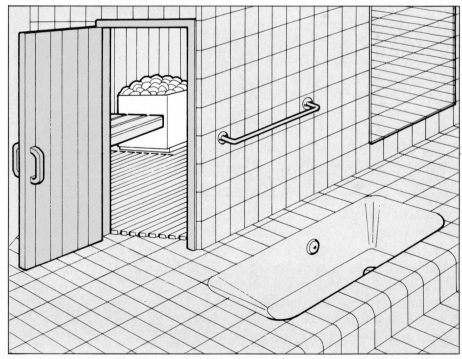

Some prefabricated stoverooms can be integrated into any indoor or outdoor installation, such as this tiled indoor spa and sauna combination.

Installing and Enjoying a Prefab Sauna

The simplest and easiest way to enjoy the bathing pleasures of Finland is to install a prefabricated modular sauna imported straight from the Old Country. For the nonhandy homeowner or the apartment dweller with little time or inclination to make capital improvements in the landlord's property, the prefab kit is ideal. Especially attractive to someone who moves a lot, this free-standing sauna can be disassembled and taken with the purchaser from home to home. It is shipped knocked down and will be delivered to your door if you can't transport it yourself. The self-contained unit can usually be assembled indoors or outdoors without any major alterations to the area where it will stand.

The complete unit contains floor, ceiling, walls, a prehung door with a window or two, benches, stove, and other optional accessories, such as bucket and ladle, vihtas, thermometer, and so forth. Some models come with a gabled roof assembly and exterior siding for outdoor use. The more elaborate designs include a dressing room, shower, and even a relaxation room with kitchen facilities. Most manufacturers of prefab saunas offer a wide variety of sizes and styles, literally dozens to choose from, so that almost any corner, room, or vacant space indoors, or any space available outdoors can be filled with an appropriate design to accommodate your family and guests.

ASSEMBLING A PREFAB SAUNA

Instructions for assembling a prefab sauna are included with each package of components. The procedure may vary from one manufacturer to another, not only in order of assembly, but in the method used to connect the parts. Before you complete the purchase of a prefab sauna, make certain that you receive printed instructions that tell you all you need to know and that the supplier or a local retailer will be able to provide you with any help you need during assembly.

All prefab saunas are assembled according to this general procedure:

- Assemble the base frame. Use a carpenter's square to make certain the corners are square. Adjust the leveling bolts.

- Raise the wall panels and the panel with the prehung door; they

ASSEMBLING A PREFAB SAUNA

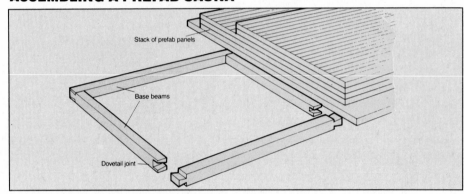

1. Assemble the base frame. Follow the manufacturer's instructions, using bolts or screws as required. Adjust the bolts that will secure the wall panels.

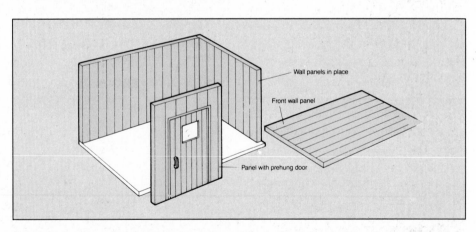

2. Raise and bolt the walls together. The wall panels and door panels are fastened together and to the base frame.

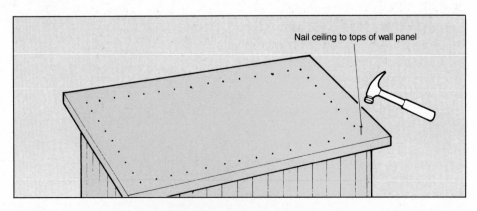

3. Attach the ceiling. The preassembled ceiling is nailed to the tops of the wall panels.

either snap, bolt, or lock together in place on the base frame and to each other.

● Nail the ceiling to the top of the wall panels.

● Attach bench cleats or supports to the side and back walls; you may have to drive screws through into the wall studs for proper support.

● Set benches and duckboard flooring into place.

● Attach the corner trim.

● Install the stove. A gas or wood-burning stove will require a flue vent. If you've chosen an electric stove, have a professional electrician make the hookup.

CURING THE SAUNA

After the sauna has been assembled properly, it is ready to be cured before using.

1. Clean up any debris accumulated during construction in the sauna itself and the surrounding area.

2. Sweep and vacuum the entire room, getting into the corners, bench supports, and under the duckboard flooring.

3. Wipe the ceiling, walls, and floor with a rag dipped in warm water.

4. Rinse off the rocks on the stove.

5. Open the door and run the heater for about 45 minutes to burn off the protective coatings. Don't be alarmed if the heater smokes during this procedure.

6. Close the door and bring the temperature up to 200 degrees Fahrenheit or 92 degrees Celsius. Within 4 or 5 hours the sauna will be ready to use.

CARING FOR THE SAUNA

Saunas are easy to take care of. With proper treatment, maintenance is practically nil.

1. After using the sauna, ventilate the room so the wood can dry out.

2. Periodically take the benches and duckboards out and hose them off.

3. Wash benches and duckboards with liquid household cleanser and rinse well to remove perspiration stains and odors.

ASSEMBLING A PREFAB SAUNA (CONTINUED)

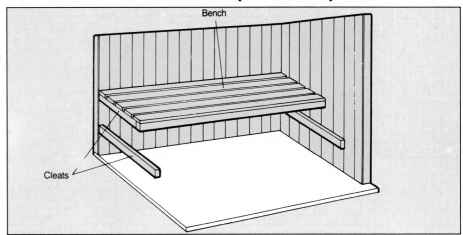

4. Install benches. Attach the bench cleats to the interior walls according to the plans. Place the benches on the cleats.

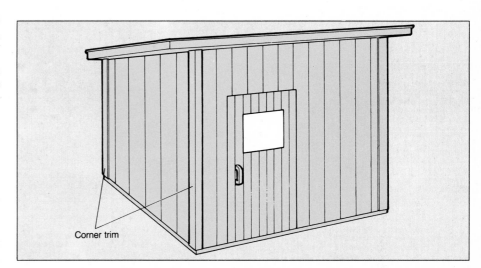

5. Attach the trim. Attach any additional trim pieces, such as corner trim, to the completed sauna building.

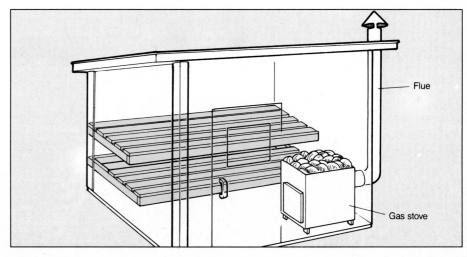

6. Install the stove. A wood-burning or gas stove will require a flue for ventilation. Electric stoves do not need one.

Installing a Sauna Indoors Step-by-Step

More and more modern homes include a sauna. Usually placed near the main bathroom or the master bedroom, it can be as large as a good-sized bathroom or as small as a linen closet. The sauna described in this project, however, is installed in a basement area as part of a renovation project to increase the recreational facilities for a growing family and their friends.

The sauna is built along a wall that used to accommodate the father's workshop and the laundry. The workshop has been moved to the garage, and new laundry facilities occupy another corner of the basement. The sauna complex includes a shower and dressing room on one side and a relaxation area complete with kitchen facilities on the other. A Ping-Pong and pool table complete the entertainment area.

The sauna stands in the dead space between two windows that remain intact for lighting and ventilation in the dressing and relaxation rooms. While these areas are rooms in their own right, the sauna itself is a large box constructed between the two areas.

There are two tiers of benches that rest on cleats fastened to the walls as runners. The two sets of benches can be arranged for an upper and lower level or placed side by side to make a double-width bench. The sauna has a prehung door complete with a long narrow window for illumination. Although a permanent wooden floor could have been built over the concrete floor, the designers decided to use the existing basement floor and cover it with movable duckboard flooring.

The interior and exterior paneling consists of red cedar planks chosen for both their decorative and aromatic qualities. The interior paneling runs horizontally, while the paneling on the exterior is cut and laid to run at a 45° angle.

The plan below shows the sauna complex described in this project. The sauna stoveroom's dimensions are 6 × 6 × 7 feet, that is a 6-foot-square room with a 7-foot ceiling. The back wall is built flush against the basement wall. The stoveroom provides for two levels of benches, an electric heater, and duckboard flooring over a concrete floor.

The relaxation and cooling-off area at the bottom of the basement stairs includes kitchen facilities, couches, and daybeds for lounging after a sauna with family or friends. On the other side of the stoveroom is a shower stall built on the site of the old laundry. Near the shower are pegs for hanging clothes, shelves to hold watches, glasses, and jewelry, and a small linen closet to store extra towels and bathrobes.

PLAN OF A BASEMENT SAUNA COMPLEX

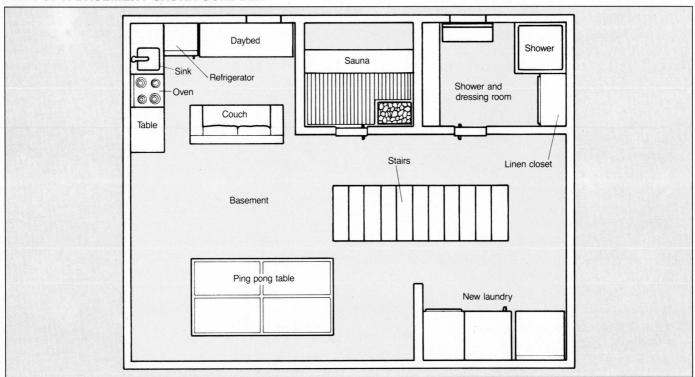

A home sauna can be the focus for a basement renovation as shown here. In most basements, plumbing facilities are already available. In this home the father's tools and workbench have been moved to the garage, thus opening up the basement.

STEP 1
FRAMING THE WALLS

Assemble four frames of 2 × 4s to the sauna dimensions, with the top and bottom plates for the side walls extending 7 inches longer than 6 feet. Cut the top and bottom plates for the front and back walls to the exact width. Cut studs 3 inches shorter than 7 feet to make room for the ceiling. Nail studs at the ends of each pair of top and bottom plates and at 24-inch intervals. Add an extra stud 2 inches inside each end stud on both side frames. Make the door space on the front frame with three studs—12 inches, 36 inches, and 60 inches from the left end. Nail a 2 × 4 header between the two studs on the left ¼ inch higher than the top of the door jamb.

STEP 2
ERECTING THE WALLS

Set the back frame against the basement wall. Plumb it with a carpenter's level and shim underneath and behind with wooden wedges until level and vertical. Toenail the top plate into the basement wall studs. If you have a concrete wall, attach the top plate with masonry nails every 18 inches. Nail the bottom plate to a wood floor with 10-penny nails, 18 inches apart. For a concrete floor, drill through the bottom plate every 18 inches with a ½-inch masonry bit. Insert ¼-inch lead anchors and attach the plate with 2½-inch screws and washers. Nail the sides to the back frame. Nail the front frame in place. Secure the two sides and front frames to the floor. Saw out the bottom plate between the doorframe studs.

STEP 3
CONSTRUCTING THE CEILING

Make a frame of 2 × 4s to the sauna dimensions. Nail 2 × 4 joists every 24 inches between the front and back plates. Sheathe one side with ¼-inch plywood. Turn it over and staple 3½-inch-thick batts of foil-faced fiberglass between the joists, foil side up. Push the batts down to leave an air pocket. Sheathe this side with ¼-inch plywood.

CONSTRUCTING THE STOVEROOM

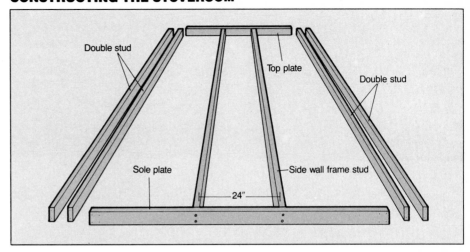

1. Lay out the wall-framing materials on the floor. Attach the top and bottom plates to the studs with 10-penny nails.

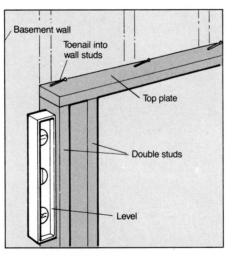

2. Frame a space for the door in the front wall frame. Nail the header to fit the door jamb.

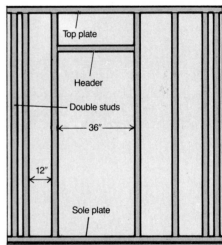

3. Use a level to set the back wall frame up vertical; toenail the top plate to the basement wall studs.

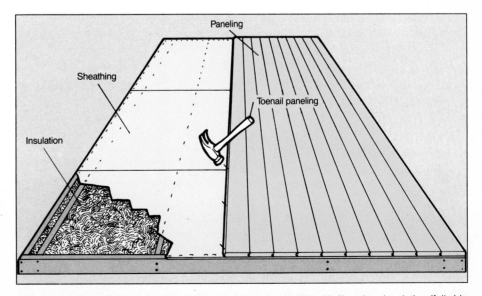

4. Assemble the ceiling upside down. Make a stud frame and fill it with fiberglass insulation (foil side toward you). Lay plywood sheathing and cover it with tongue-in-groove paneling.

Lay tongue-and-groove panels over the sheath at right angles to the joists. Set the first panel with the groove edge flush with the frame edge. Facenail it with four 8-penny nails. Countersink nails at 45-degree angles through the base of the tongue and into each joist. Nail other panels only through the tongue for a clean look. On the last board, cut the tongue edge to within ½ inch of the frame edge; nail in place.

STEP 4
ADDING THE CEILING

Drill two ¼-inch holes in the top plate of each wall frame about one-third of the way from each end. Next, align the ceiling on the top of the wall frames. Make sure the paneled side of the ceiling faces down into the interior of the stoveroom. When the ceiling is perfectly in place, drill ³⁄₁₆-inch holes into the ceiling frame by inserting the drill through the ¼-inch holes in the top plate of each wall frame. Use ¼-inch lag screws 3 inches long and washers to secure the ceiling to the walls.

STEP 5
RUNNING ELECTRICAL POWER

Run a heat-resistant cable from a nearby junction box to the place in the front wall frame behind which the heater will be placed. If you are leading the cable in from the basement ceiling, drill a ¾-inch hole through the sauna's ceiling and the top plate of the front wall frame near the stud that is closest to the location of the heater. Then the cable can be threaded through the ceiling and front wall frame (for anchoring) and dropped down the exterior of the front wall to the hole near the heater, where it can be led back into the interior of the stoveroom for connection to the stove.

STEP 6
INSULATING THE WALLS

Assemble sufficient foil-faced fiberglass insulation batts to line all walls of the stoveroom. Always wear protective clothing when working with fiberglass insulation to prevent the fibers

CONSTRUCTING THE STOVEROOM (CONTINUED)

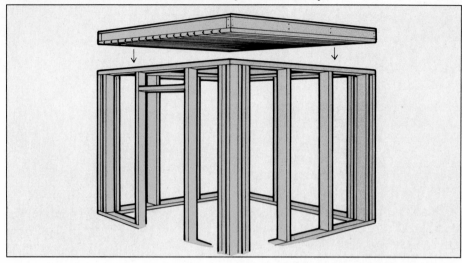

5. With a helper or two, lift the ceiling up onto the wall frames and attach it securely to the walls with 3-inch lag screws.

WIRING THE SAUNA

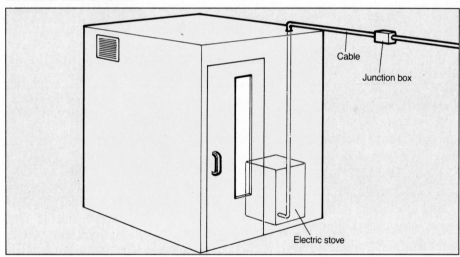

Use only heat-resistant cables for wiring a sauna; run them from the nearest junction box through the wall of the sauna.

INSULATING THE WALLS

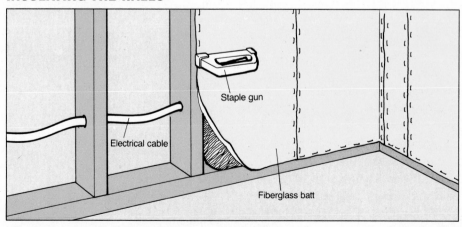

Fiberglass batts come in standard sizes to fit easily between wall studs. Trim them with heavy-duty scissors if necessary.

from irritating your skin. Working in one direction around the perimeter of the stoveroom, staple the flanges of the insulation batts to the wall studs so that the foil side faces into the room. This will enable the foil to act as a vapor barrier, keeping moisture from getting into the insulation and the exterior wall surface. The foil will also reflect heat back into the stoveroom.

STEP 7
PROVIDING EXTERIOR VENTS AND SHEATHING

Cut a hole for an intake vent in the wall behind the stove about 6 inches from the floor, and a second hole for an exhaust vent a few inches from the ceiling on the opposite wall. Check your building department codes for the proper vent area for your sauna. Typically, the total vent area should be about ½0 the floor area (never less than 1½ square feet). Two 11-inch-square holes would provide the minimum amount. Sheathe the exterior of the sauna with wallboard and cut holes for the vents. Later cover the vent holes with metal vent plates. The interior plate for the exhaust vent (installed after paneling) should be adjustable.

STEP 8
PANELING INTERIOR AND EXTERIOR WALLS

To panel horizontally, measure the wall's height and divide by the panel's width to find the number of boards. Use tongue-and-groove panels. Lay the first panel at the bottom, groove side down, and attach to the studs with 8-penny nails. Then countersink nails through the tongue and proceed up to the ceiling. Cut holes for the vents before you attach those panels. Cut the top panel along the back edge of the tongue side at a 45-degree angle to fit snugly against the ceiling. Panel the exterior walls similarly. To panel at a 45-degree angle, the first piece of paneling must be triangular to fit in the lower corner of the wall. Use a T-square to draw each angle and cut to fit. Proceed as above.

SHEATHING AND PANELING THE WALLS

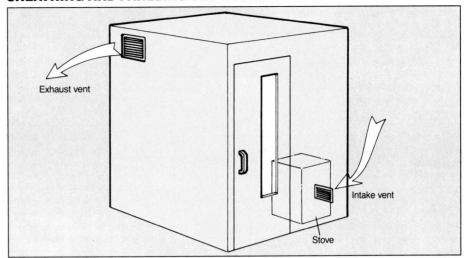

1. Sheathe the exterior of the sauna with wallboard and cut appropriate holes through it and the insulation for vents.

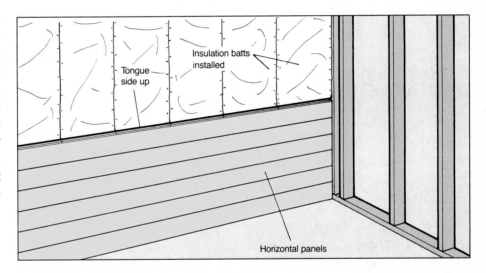

2. When measuring for the number of paneling boards you'll need, if the last board at the top of a wall will be less than half a width, increase it to a full half-width and cut the amount of increase from the groove side of the first board laid at the bottom.

BUILDING THE BENCHES

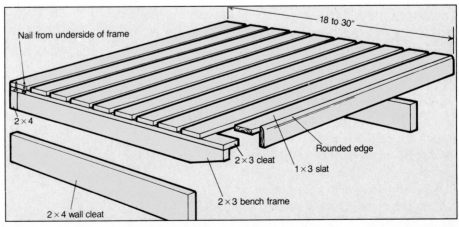

Assemble the benches by nailing through the cleats into the slats; make sure the nailheads do not protrude. The bench frames must be square to sit steady on the wall cleats.

STEP 9
BUILDING THE BENCHES

Cut three 2 × 3s as long as the width of the bench to use as bench cleats. Then cut as many 1 × 3s as you need to form the lengthwise slats for the seating surface; allow for slight gaps between each slat. Each slat should be cut ¼ inch shorter than the bench is long. Smooth and round the top edges of the slats with sandpaper so they will be comfortable to sit on. Lay the slats on the floor, broadside up. Lay the cleats across them, one on each end and one across the middle. Space the slats evenly with a slight gap between them. Nail through the cleats so that the nailheads are on the underside of the frame. Make a similar seat for the other tier. Set the seats upon the cleats but do not nail them down.

STEP 10
INSTALLING THE BENCHES

Construct 2 × 4 wall cleats to go along the interior back and side walls of the stoveroom, one set of cleats to support an upper tier and another to support a lower tier. The side-wall cleats for the lower tier should be cut twice the width of the bench itself with ½ inch to spare. The side-wall cleats for the upper tier can be cut one bench-width long. Fasten the cleats securely with long wood screws driven into the wall studs at heights of 32 inches for the top tier and 16 inches for the lower.

STEP 11
INSTALLING A PREHUNG DOOR

Set the door and jamb in the roughed-out door opening. Wedge pieces of cardboard between the jamb and the studs to hold it in place temporarily. Slip two wood shims of equal thickness between the top of the jamb and the header beam. Space them evenly. Insert three similar shims on each side of the jamb to create a ¼-inch clearance around the jamb. On the hinge side, place a shim just below each hinge and a third centered between the hinges. Secure the door jamb with 10-penny

INSTALLING THE BENCHES

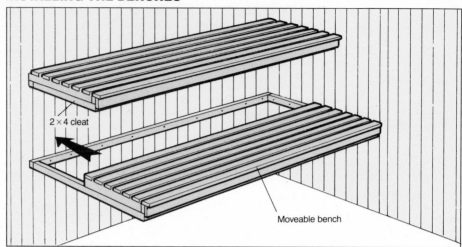

Mount the 2 × 4 wall cleats securely with long wood screws to the stud walls. Make sure they are level and at the appropriate heights before fastening them to the walls.

FITTING THE DOOR

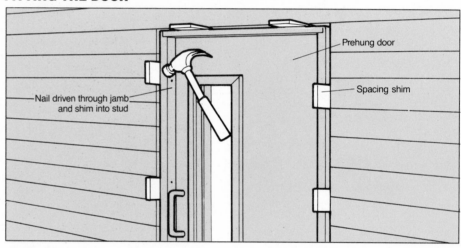

Be sure the door fits well so that heat will not be lost around the doorframe. When the door is in place, the protruding shims can either be sawed off or knocked off with a hammer. Sauna doors must open outward for safety.

GUARDING THE STOVE

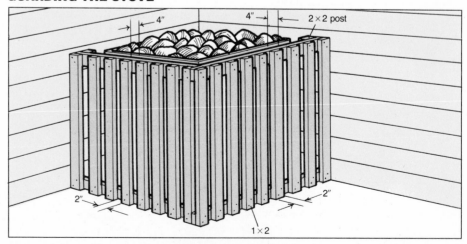

Although not all manufacturer's instructions call for it, a simple picket fence around the stove is a good safety precaution, psychologically removing the stove from the area where bathers walk. It can be made easily from 1 × 2s nailed to 2 × 2 posts.

nails driven through the jamb, the shims, and into the studs that frame the door. Saw off the protruding ends of the shims and remove the cardboard wedging. Finish the doorway with interior and exterior door casings.

STEP 12
INSTALLING THE STOVE

Install the stove according to the manufacturer's instructions. For safety, enclose it in a small picket fence. Cut a pair of 1×2s for fence rails to reach from the side wall to 4 inches beyond the heater. Lay them parallel on the floor, as far apart as the distance from the floor to the top of the rock heap on the stove. Cut more 1×2s for pickets and nail one on each end of the rails and the others spaced evenly between them. Build a second section of fence to fit the narrower distance to the other wall. Attach two fence posts made of 2×2s to each wall at the point where the fence will be attached. Nail the rails to the posts and to each other at the corner.

STEP 13
DUCKBOARD FLOORING

If you plan to use a lot of water in your sauna, you may want to slope the floor slightly and install a drain. But with or without the drain, wooden duckboard flooring over concrete or tile is pleasant to walk on and can be easily removed for cleaning. Nail four 2×2s or 2×3s together in a frame measured to fit easily into the sauna and cover the most walked-over part of the floor. Cut 1×3s and sand the top edges smooth. Nail them to the frame from the underside, leaving a ½-inch space between them.

STEP 14
FRAMING THE SHOWER STALL

Construct the framing for the shower stall according to the size of the stall purchased; the one shown here is 36 inches. Dig the drain hole 18 inches from the back wall and centered between the side walls. Apply blocking 78½ inches high to provide a nailing

MAKING SAFE FLOOR COVERINGS

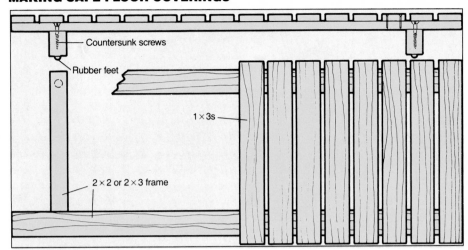

Duckboards are racks of wooden strips with narrow spaces between them used for floor coverings where water would tend to make the actual floor surface slippery to walk on. They are easily constructed out of a frame of 2×2s covered with 1×3s.

CONSTRUCTING THE SHOWER STALL

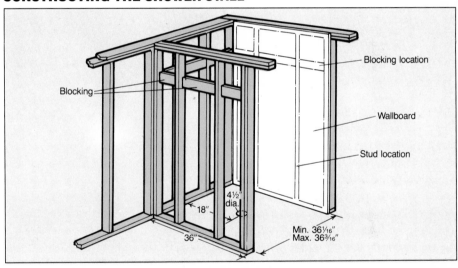

1. The stud framing is set up to fit exactly the shower stall itself. When you install the wallboard, mark the location of the studs and the blocking so you can find them later.

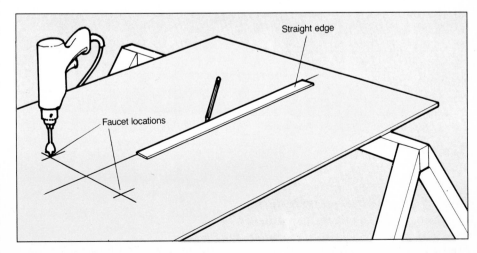

2. Place the side wall panel on sawhorses and rough in the showerhead and the faucets. Drill slightly oversized holes with a spade bit.

surface for the wallboard. Mount the wallboard (or tile backer board) to provide a bearing surface for the shower walls. The wallboard will also help quiet the drumming noise that occurs when water hits the fiberglass shell. Cut 2×4s or 2×6s 12 inches longer than the grab bars and attach these to the studs.

STEP 15
PREPARING FOR THE FIXTURES

The drain line must project ½ inch above floor. Rough in water-supply lines. The faucets should be centered on the center line of the front wall. Valves should be no higher than 4 feet from the floor. The showerhead should be no less than 72 inches from floor, that is, immediately above the blocking. Place the side wall that will have valves into position and mark holes. Cut them with a spade bit or a hole saw. Remove the wall till later.

STEP 16
FIXING THE DRAIN AND SHOWER PAN

If you're not sure of the plumbing code in your locality, check with authorities first. If you are following an old plumbing code, use oakum and lead to seal the drain and allow the ½-inch projection of the drain line to remain. Newer codes permit a plastic seal that requires only a ⅛-inch projection. Sweep the floor clean of all debris and set the shower pan in place. Level it, shimming under the legs and ribs. Nail the pan to the studs with big-head roofing nails. Protect the fiberglass surface with a section of cardboard. Make sure you don't hit the surface of the shower pan with the hammer.

STEP 17
INSTALLING THE SHOWER WALLS

Clean the sealant grooves on the three upper edges of the shower pan with a brush or a vacuum. Use the sealant provided with the shower kit. Run a bead of sealant in the groove at the

CONSTRUCTING THE SHOWER STALL (CONTINUED)

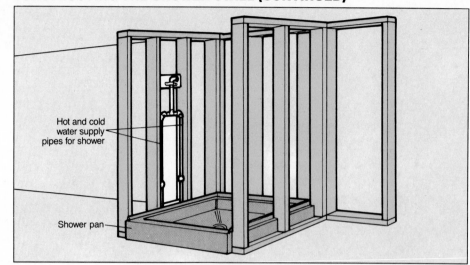

Hot and cold water supply pipes for shower

Shower pan

3. Be sure the drain and shower pan are level and free of leaks. From here on, it will be harder to make corrections.

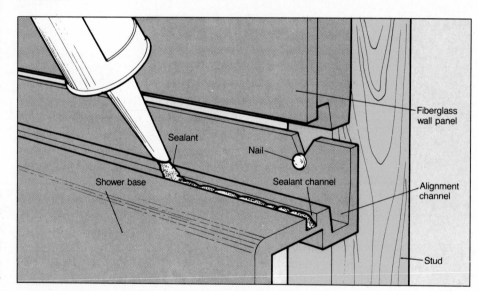

Sealant

Nail

Shower base

Sealant channel

Fiberglass wall panel

Alignment channel

Stud

4. The sealant holds the walls firmly in their proper channel and prevents water from running down behind the wall panels.

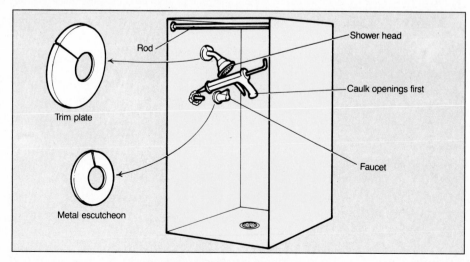

Rod

Trim plate

Metal escutcheon

Shower head

Caulk openings first

Faucet

5. After installing faucets and showerhead, caulk around them to keep moisture from getting behind the walls.

back of the shower. Set the back wall in place and seat it firmly in the groove. Do not fasten it yet. Apply sealant to the vertical channels in the back wall and to the horizontal channels at the sides of the shower pan. Place the side walls into the grooves and seat them firmly. Use a damp cloth to wipe off excess sealant. Shim the back wall at its upper edge to bring the vertical edge of the back wall firmly against the side walls. Shim the side walls to make them plumb and square with the pan. Fasten the walls to the studs and blocking with the screws supplied.

STEP 18
INSTALLING THE FIXTURES
Install the faucets and caulk the openings before attaching the escutcheons around the faucet stems. Caulk around the stem of the showerhead and install the trim plate provided with it. You can install a shower door or attach a simple rod to the wall surface and hang a curtain for privacy.

STEP 19
BUILDING THE STOVEROOM DOOR
The stoveroom door is a critical part of an efficient unit. Since taking a sauna includes sessions inside the stoveroom alternating with showering and cooling off outside, there can be a lot of coming and going in a single bath. If too much heat escapes, the full effect of the dry-heat bath is lost. For this reason, the stoveroom door is traditionally small and narrow.

Some build-it-yourselfers install exceptionally small doors, for example 3½ feet by 4 feet. They claim that the twisting to get in and out is worth the heat that is saved. This trapdoor style is also easy and inexpensive to build. A large door may reach as high as 6 feet 5 inches. The extra height allows the width to be reduced to as little as 20 to 24 inches since there is no need to bend to get through. While the total door space determines how much heat escapes, a high door will let heat out from near the ceiling where it is hottest. For this reason, the door should be as low as possible, given your preference.

The sauna door should have no locks or catches that could accidentally stick and trap someone inside, and it should swing outward for the bathers' convenience. A roller-ball catch set into the jamb makes a suitable catch. A door will shrink and swell as the temperature changes. Be sure your door fits just right or it may leak heat or get stuck. You can buy prehung sauna doors from sauna manufacturers for a home-built sauna or you can make your own. If you build your own, follow this procedure:

● Make a frame of 2 × 4s to the desired size.
● Sheathe the exterior side with plywood.
● Flip the door over and install batts of insulation, foil side up.
● Panel the interior side with the same type of wood that you will use for the interior walls. Tongue-and-groove

BUILDING THE STOVEROOM DOOR

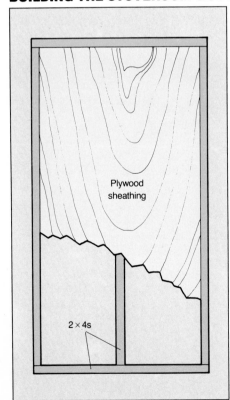

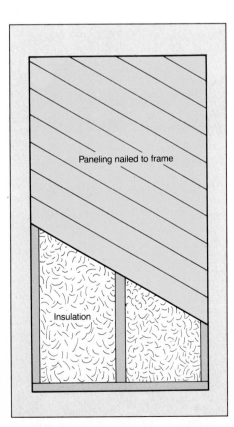

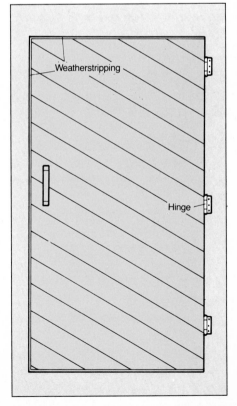

1. Make the frame. Cut 2 × 4s to make a frame that will just fill the space required. Cover the exterior side of the frame with plywood.

2. Add insulation and paneling. Lay insulation batts inside the frame and cover it with paneling.

3. Install the door. Hang the door on three hinges to the door frame. Seal the door opening with weatherstripping. Install handles.

panels are best for a tight seal.

● Attach a wooden handle to each side.

● Set the door with three fence hinges.

● Attach strips of foam weatherproofing along the doorframe.

STEP 20
CONVERTING A SOLID-CORE DOOR

Another option when building the stoveroom door is to buy a solid-core door at a hardware store or lumberyard and convert it yourself with a little insulation. Simply follow this procedure:

● Cut furring strips to run the length of the door on each side of the door. Angle the exterior side of the strip to fit the doorjamb.

● Attach top and bottom caps to the furring strips flush with the top and bottom of the door.

● Install foil-faced insulation on the inside of the door between the furring strips, foil side up; that is, away from the door, to protect the door from moisture.

● Cover the insulation with appropriate paneling nailed to the furring strips.

STEP 21
CUTTING A WINDOW IN A DOOR

Often the door window is the only window in the stoveroom. Since the stoveroom should have subdued lighting to encourage peaceful relaxation, a small window in the door is all that is needed. Here's how to cut and install a window in a solid-core door:

● Cut a hole 1 foot square in the center of the door.

● Frame the hole on both sides of the door with 1 × 3s.

● Set a pane of glass in the 1 × 1 foot cutout.

● Use quarter round on each side to hold the glass in place.

● To keep the window in an outdoor sauna from steaming up in cold weather, install a double pane of glass with an air pocket between the two panes.

CONVERTING A SOLID CORE DOOR

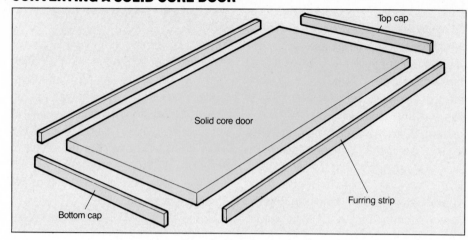

1. Attach furring. Install furring strips all around the door to create a trough to hold the insulation.

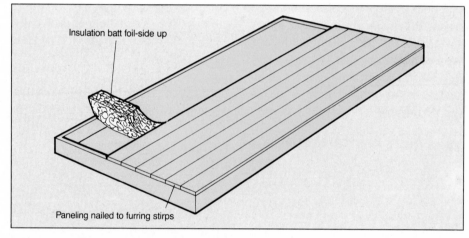

2. Install insulation and paneling. Lay insulation batts inside the furring strips and nail paneling over the batts and to the strips.

CUTTING AND FRAMING A WINDOW

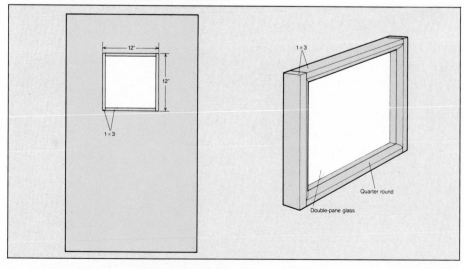

A small 1 × 1-foot window cut into a solid-core door will admit light and prevent the feeling of claustrophobia in the stoveroom.

STEP 22
THE "CLOSET STOVEROOM" OPTION

Although this project calls for the construction of all stoveroom walls, many people convert large closets or unused pantries into sauna stoverooms by using the existing framework and studs for the walls of the stoveroom.

If you have a suitably large and well-constructed closet or pantry, you· can turn it into an indoor sauna stoveroom easily and inexpensively. Simply attach fiberglass batts of insulation (foil side facing you) to the wall studs and cover them with paneling. Lower and insulate the ceiling like the walls.

If you choose to build a sauna in this way, you'll want to reframe the door so that it will be smaller and more efficient. Reframe the doorway (and lower the ceiling, if necessary) before you do any other work.

Here is the general procedure for reframing a closet or pantry doorway to make it a proper stoveroom doorway:

1. Remove the jamb, jack studs, header, and cripple studs of the old door.

2. Measure inward from each wall stud the distance needed to reduce the doorway, allowing for the width.of the new door jamb.

3. Measure downward from the top plate of the wall the distance needed to lower the height of the door, factoring in the width of the new doorjamb.

4. For each side of the door, construct a 2×4 frame whose width will reduce the door opening one half the desired amount and whose height will lower the door to the acceptable height. Use 2×4s for the sides of each frame and for the bottom plate. Do not attach a header beam across the top at this point.

5. Nail each frame to the wall studs and attach a 2×4 across the top of them to serve as a header.

6. Add cripple studs above the new header at each end and one or two in the middle.

7. Install the new door and jamb.

REFRAMING A CLOSET DOOR

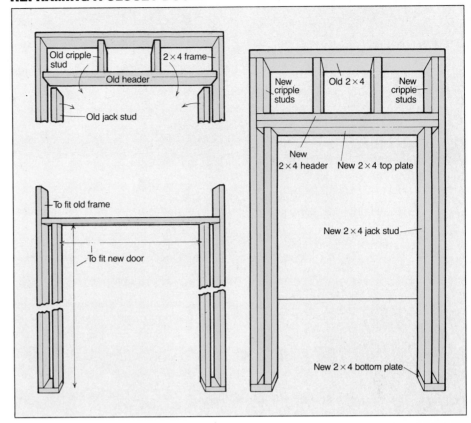

First remove the old door, jack studs, header, and cripple studs, leaving a clean 2×4 frame. Then cut new studs and a top plate to make a frame whose inside dimensions accommodate the smaller sauna door, as shown at left. Install this frame in the old door frame and cut a new header and cripple studs to fill the remaining space above the new frame.

COMPLETED BASEMENT SAUNA PROJECT

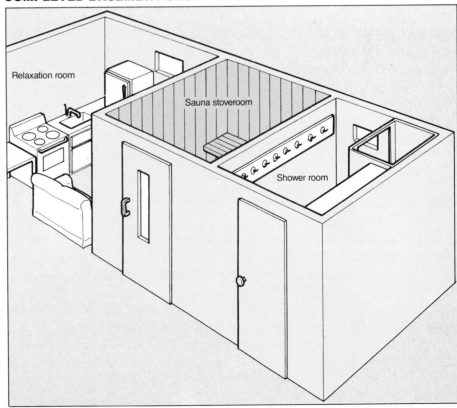

Planning a Sauna Project

The first step in any construction planning is to check with your local building department to see what permits you'll need. Regulations, in theory, ensure you and the community safe and long-lasting construction, although some of them may be a nuisance. They may specify measurements and materials for foundations, framing, insulation. and wiring. Zoning laws that cover property use specify the size and type of structures that may be added to residential property, and even the function of such buildings. It's important to know, for example, how far back from the property line an outdoor sauna must be sited. If you want a variance in order to deviate from the local code, apply for it. Minor deviations are often readily granted. You may be granted major variances, but they will have to be decided by an appeal board.

STEP 1
SKETCHING THE PROJECT
In planning a project, it's important to get your ideas down on paper and discover your limitations and assets, figure out your options, and avoid unpleasant surprises later. Having your project sketched out will give you confidence and ensure that you've considered all the practical and aesthetic factors that will influence your design.

Start by making a Venn diagram. This is a sketch that represents the major areas of your project by rough overlapping circles. In this case, sketch in the sauna stoveroom and dressing area in relation to the rest of the bathroom and bedroom complex. You might also consider whether you'll need a special storage area or additional linen closet. If you are installing a sauna in the basement, make your sketch indicate that the stoveroom is to be placed near the tank or shower, and the relaxation room is to be near the dressing room. Let the shower share

plumbing lines with a small kitchenette in the relaxation room. Sketch a basement sauna in relationship to plumbing, drains, windows, traffic patterns, and other present basement areas.

If your sauna is to be located outside, use Venn circles to sketch other structures and facilities on your property: the house, garage, drive, utility lines, trees, fences, shrubs, and other structures. Note any slope to the property that would allow drainage. You'll want overflow from your shower or tank room to run away from the sauna and not collect under it. If you have a swimming pool, you can use it for cooling off.

STEP 2
MAKING A SCALE PLAN
Once you have the major areas roughed in, draw a scale plan of your property on graph paper, including utility lines and hook-ups as well as other structures, and indicate privacy factors and the view from the sauna window. At this point you can begin to estimate and then refine the size of respective rooms in the sauna complex. Two popular sizes for stoverooms are $5 \times 7 \times 7$ feet and $6 \times 6 \times 7$ feet. Keep in mind that internal walk space should be kept to a minimum to allow for as many seating and reclining areas as possible. Decide on the layout of benches, how many tiers you'll have, if any, and the location of the stove.

STEP 3
STAKING OUT THE CORNERS
Locate the exact points for the four corners by placing stakes and using string to scribe arcs. Place the first stake in one corner designated A. Place the second stake at corner B. Use two strings, one the length of A-C attached to corner B, and the other the length of the diagonal B-C attached to corner A, to scribe arcs. The point where they intersect is corner D.

MAKING A VENN DIAGRAM

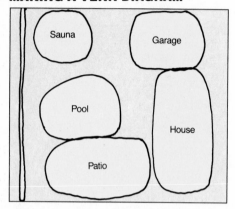

In this Venn diagram, the basic areas of the site are represented by rough circles.

MAKING A SCALE DRAWING

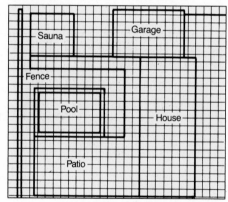

Transfer Venn diagram for sauna to scale drawing on graph paper to find actual measurements.

STAKING THE FOUNDATION

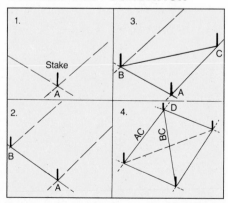

Measure diagonal strings in place. If foundation corners are square, diagonals will be equal.

Forming and Pouring Footings

If you plan to build an outdoor sauna from the ground up, you may want to construct a concrete footing as a foundation. After all, the sauna will become as important a structure as any other outdoor building and may become the family's favorite place to rest and relax even when not enjoying the sauna.

Not every outdoor sauna requires a concrete foundation, however. If the ground is hard and well packed, you can sink concrete building blocks into the dirt, allowing 1 to 2 inches to protrude above ground. A frame of 2 × 4s covered with heavy plywood and secured to the concrete blocks may be all you need for a simple sauna consisting of a stoveroom and nothing else. The outside area where the tank and resting benches are could be a deck or a floor made of walnut stumps. It's a bit rustic, but many people in warmer climates prefer such simplicity to an elaborately built structure.

On the other hand, if you need to come to terms with a harsher climate, you'll want a substantial sauna with a solid foundation and an insulated floor. The shape and size will vary according to the type of sauna complex you are building, but the generalized procedure is as follows.

STEP 1
SETTING UP BATTER BOARDS
After you square the stakes and the string, as described on page 108, take three 2 × 4 stakes 24 inches long and drive them into the ground just outside the corner stakes you have set. Nail 1 × 4 batter boards approximately 5 to 6 feet long to the stakes so that the top of each is 12 inches above ground. Level the boards, making sure each corner is the same elevation. Then check them with a carpenter's level to make sure they are true as well as level. String lines from board to board so they cross over the initial corner stakes that you

PLACING BATTER BOARDS

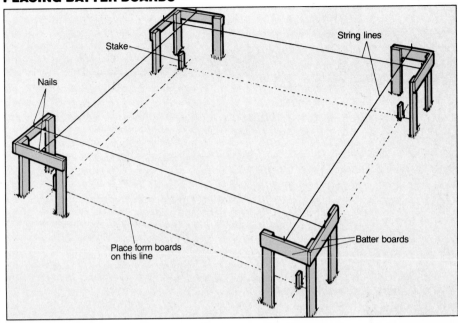

Set up batter boards a few inches outside your first stakes, as shown above. Make sure they're level. Secure lines to nails and run them between the boards so that they cross above the first stakes.

SETTING UP THE FORMS

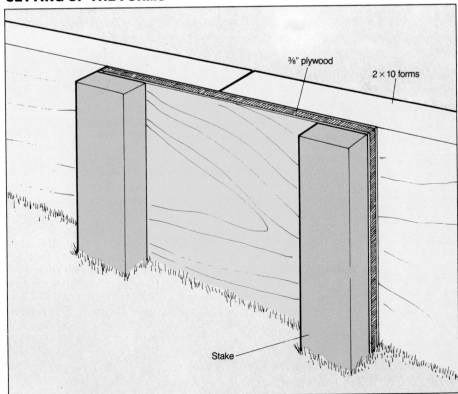

1. Back the 2 × 10 form boards with 2 × 4 stakes. Each joint requires an additional piece of plywood behind it and two stakes.

drove in while staking out the area. Connect the lines to nails in the top of the batter boards. Check dimensions again and remove the corner stakes.

STEP 2
MAKING THE FORMS

Once you have staked out the true dimensions of the foundation and erected string guides that are level, install the forms for the concrete. Set 8-foot sections of 2 × 10s on edge under the string. Align the inner face of each board with the string. Reinforce each section of board with four stakes made of 2 × 4s. Make sure that each joint will have an additional stake on either side with a ⅜-inch plywood piece as a backup board. Nail all the form boards to the stakes. Use double-headed nails or leave the nail heads exposed to make removing the forms easier. Complete the entire perimeter this way.

STEP 3
BRACING THE FORMS

Brace the form boards to keep them from moving when you pour the concrete. Drive another 2 × 4 stake 12 inches behind each stake supporting the form. Nail 1 × 2s at bottom and top to form a triangular brace. Check all dimensions and levels again. It will be too late to check if everything is square and level after you pour the concrete.

STEP 4
EXCAVATING THE TRENCH

When the forms are complete, dig a trench inside the forms to make the extra thickness to the slab edge. Use the face of the form as a guide for the wall of the trench. The trench should be 12 inches wide and 16 inches deep. When the trench is dug, taper the inner sides by shaving 6 inches away from the inside top of the trench. Angle this cut downward so the bottom of the trench remains 12 inches wide. Next drive a pair of ⅝-inch deformed reinforcing bars 6 inches apart every 24 to 48 inches on center. The bars should extend up to 3 inches below the top of the form boards.

SETTING UP THE FORMS (CONTINUED)

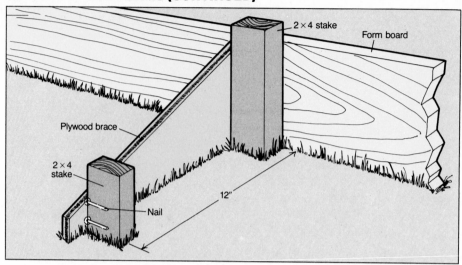

2. For added support, brace the form boards with triangular fittings to keep the boards from bending during the pour.

DIGGING THE FOUNDATION TRENCH

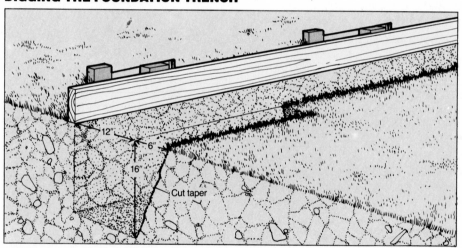

Dig the trench around the foundation 6 inches wider at the inside top than at the bottom by tapering the side of the trench.

PLACING REINFORCING BARS

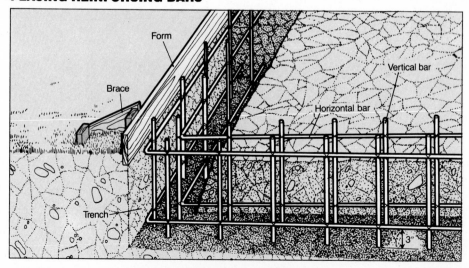

Tie two rows of reinforcing bars to the vertical bars with wire at each juncture. Be certain that the reinforcing does not move.

STEP 5
PLACING REINFORCING RODS

To form the horizontal reinforcing rods in the trench, buy two ⅝-inch rods that are 6 inches shorter than the length of the form so that the form extends 3 inches on either side. Place horizontal rods on the outside of the vertical rods and tie them to the verticals with tying wire. Set the bottom rods at least 3 inches above the bottom of the trench. Do this in all the trenches. Overlap the rods at corners and wire them together. Repeat this procedure for the top horizontal rod, installing it around the perimeter 3 inches below the top of the form boards. All horizontal steel should be in place and well tied so the framework does not move.

STEP 6
LAYING THE GRAVEL BASE

When the rods are in place, pour a 4-inch layer of clean gravel with no aggregate larger than 1 inch over the flat portion of the excavated ground. Don't let gravel fall into the trenches. Place a 6-mil polyethylene sheet or vapor barrier over the leveled gravel and lay welded wire fabric on top. Tie the fabric to the horizontal rods with tie wire.

STEP 7
PLACING THE CONCRETE

Pour concrete into the form and move it into the trenches and all nooks and crannies. When the form is full, screed the surface using a length of 2×4. Move the wood back and forth across the top of the forms until the concrete is level and smooth. Spray the forms and concrete with water beginning the day after you pour the concrete, to produce a stronger slab. Continue to keep the concrete damp while it cures for 3 days.

STEP 8
REMOVING THE FORMS

Strip the forms at the end of the second complete day of curing. The concrete will still be green, which is its usual coloration during curing. Try not to hit the concrete with a sledgehammer when you remove the wood forms.

LAYING THE GRAVEL BASE

The base of the foundation is a layer of gravel over which a sheet of plastic is placed, topped with welded wire fabric.

PLACING THE CONCRETE

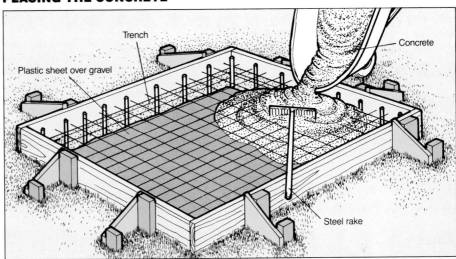

Mix and pour the concrete, moving it evenly into the wire mesh, down into the trench, and into all the crevices with a sturdy steel rake.

REMOVING THE FORMS

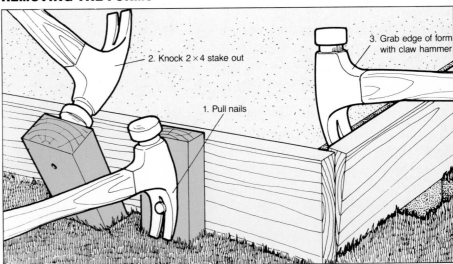

The final step at the end of the second day of curing is to remove the form boards carefully so as not to disturb the slab.

Building Framing for a Sauna Complex

STEP 1
MAKING THE FRAMES

Lay out 2 × 4s for framing the longest wall in its entirety. Arrange 2 × 4 studs within the frame so that they measure 16 inches on center. Lay out window and door frames by attaching headers where they are needed; nail together.

STEP 2
RAISING THE FRAMES

Lift the frame into place and nail the sole plate to the sill. Brace the wall with 2 × 4s nailed to the frame until the next wall is raised. Frame the entire outside wall in one section even if the sauna will be divided into several rooms. Lay out and frame the partition walls after the entire four exterior walls are up.

STEP 3
FINISHING THE WALL FRAMES

When all the walls are raised, join the corners in one of the two ways shown here. Make sure the walls are plumb; cap the wall frames with 2 × 4s.

STEP 4
CONSTRUCTING THE ROOF

Ask a local builder what the most effective roof pitch is for your locality, and plan for a 1-foot overhang. To frame a roof, toenail ceiling joists to the wall plate and the center partition wall. These can be spaced 24 inches apart since there will not be a room above the ceiling. The joists brace the rafters and hold the walls together. Erect rafters in pairs by toenailing them to wall plates and facenailing them to ceiling joists and the center ridgeboard. If the pitch of the roof is exceptionally high, brace each pair of rafters with a collar beam.

STEP 5
INSTALLING GABLE STUDS

Measure and cut gable studs. Toenail them to wall plates and facenail them to the end rafters.

CONSTRUCTING THE FRAMING

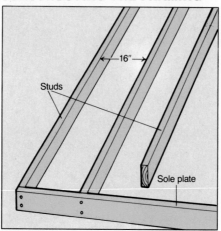

1. Lay out the studs so that they measure 16 inches on center.

2. You will probably need some help to raise the walls. Rough-nail 2 × 4s to each end to brace it.

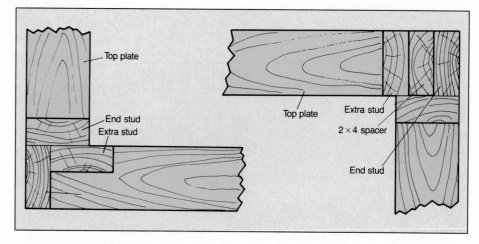

3. Here are two methods for joining corners. The right one is typical in older houses, the left more common in modern buildings. In both, all the studs are nailed together to make a strong corner.

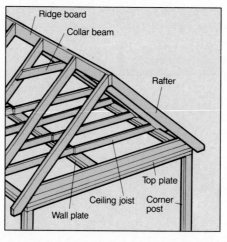

4. First, nail joists across the erected wall frames. Then toenail rafters in pairs to wall plates and facenail to joists.

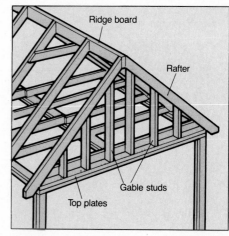

5. Measure the various lengths for gable or cripple studs. Cut and toenail them to the top wall plate and the gable rafter.

Installing a Sauna Outdoors Step-by-Step

An outdoor sauna complex makes the ideal setting for sauna bathing. The physical detachment of the sauna complex from the house itself helps bathers to detach themselves psychologically from any reminders of everyday life. Regardless of climate, an outdoor sauna stoveroom provides a warm, year-round haven for the world-weary; and a cold-water area, even if it is outdoors and the day is chilly, offers a refreshingly invigorating contrast. Consider the fact that sauna bathing originated outdoors, not far from the Arctic Circle!

The only drawbacks to an outdoor sauna complex are that the extra insulation and amenities required will make it relatively expensive to build, and that it may take up more room than you are willing to sacrifice if your yard

space is limited. If your climate is very mild, the outdoor complex may cost no more to build than an indoor one. It may, in fact, be less expensive if you decide on a very simple approach. As for yard size, it's just a matter of personal aesthetics: a sauna complex can take up as little as 6 square feet, including stoveroom, clothes locker, and outdoor shower.

When building an outdoor sauna complex as a self-contained cottage, complete with stoveroom, shower, dressing room, and relaxation area, you have a wide range of options, for the detached sauna unit can be as elaborate or as primitive as you wish. You are, in effect, constructing a small building. The possibilities are limited only by your imagination and finances. You may want to include an ultrasleek

sauna complex in a large cabaña or outbuilding attached to a pool surround, or you may want to tuck a small chalet-style sauna complex in the middle of a group of fir trees.

The instructions for an outdoor sauna project that appear in this section are necessarily general, since you will want your final design to reflect your personal taste and to be in harmony with the surrounding environment. The instructions will, however, provide you with some basic considerations for building any type of outdoor sauna.

The plan below describes a very rustic sauna complex that features a stoveroom with a wood-burning stove, a dressing shed, an adjacent cooling-off tank, and a surrounding fence that ensures privacy and creates a windbreak.

PLAN OF AN OUTDOOR SAUNA COMPLEX

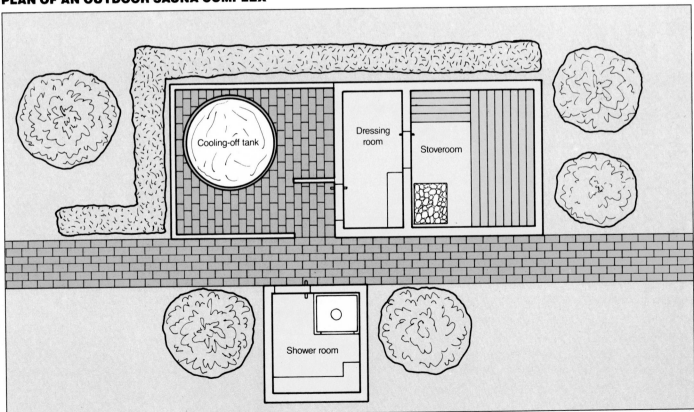

The outdoor sauna project, shown above, separates the facilities into two buildings, the one at the top containing the stoveroom and dressing room, and a smaller shower building across the walk. A cooling-off tank is convenient to both.

STEP 1
CONCRETE FOOTINGS AND PILINGS

Ask your local building department about the most secure footing for the size of the sauna complex you plan to construct, and for the type of soil you are building on. Since a sauna complex typically involves a small building (sometimes little more than a stove-room, as in this plan) and since that building is used for rather gentle activities, you need not overbuild your foundation. Climate is also an important factor to consider, especially if you experience freezing topsoil, low winter temperatures, and strong winds. These conditions may require that you install extra-tight insulation between the sauna floor and the ground.

Concrete pilings are an alternative to pouring solid foundations. Simply mark and dig holes for the pilings, determining the number and arrangement according to professional advice from local contractors or building inspectors. You can use cardboard boxes for forms, letting them protrude a good 18 inches above ground. Mix and pour the concrete, sinking J-bolts into the fresh concrete, to which you attach the sill plate later. When the concrete has set, tear away the cardboard forms.

On solid soil, simple concrete blocks may be all that is needed, positioned correctly and set partway into the ground.

Remember that any wood that comes into contact with the ground should be treated against termites to prevent moisture rot.

STEP 2
RAILROAD TIE FOUNDATION

An easy foundation to install is one made of railroad ties, which you can often buy from local railroad yards at salvage prices. Lay the ties on flat earth, firmly embedded in the dirt and secured to each other with hinges. Fill the area inside the ties with gravel and insulate with a layer of polyethylene that covers both the gravel and the ties. Add a second layer of gravel over the

CONCRETE PILING FOUNDATION

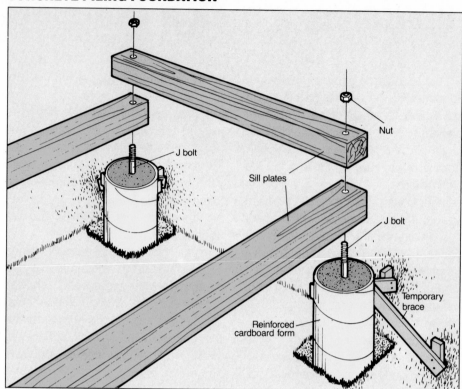

Concrete pilings can be made by pouring concrete into reinforced cardboard forms, which are peeled off when the concrete is dry.

RAILROAD TIE FOUNDATION

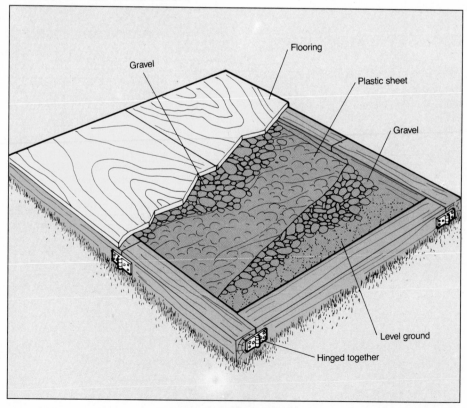

If the earth is firm and solid, a simple square of railroad ties filled with two layers of gravel makes a good foundation.

plastic sheet for the floor and cover the area with wooden duckboard flooring. The entire foundation will provide good drainage and excellent insulation. Nail the wall studs directly to the ties.

STEP 3
INSULATING FLOORS

The most popular and traditional floor is wood and for a good reason: wood is a natural insulator. The standard wooden floor for an outdoor sauna stoveroom has several basic parts. First, construct a frame with joists out of 2 × 4s. On the bottom of the frame, nail sheets of a water-sealant material such as waxed cardboard. Above this sheathing lay batts of foil-covered fiberglass insulation, with the foil side facing up into the room. A top layer of polyethylene-coated-cardboard stretched across the joists completes the floor structure. Simply cover the top with 1-inch plywood, nailed to the joists, and you have the floor. Duckboards can be added.

STEP 4
INSULATING WALLS

Tack sheets of aluminum foil 1 mil thick to the outer studs of the stoveroom walls—just inside the exterior paneling—to create a vapor barrier that will retain heat emanating from the interior. Staple foil-covered fiberglass 3¼ inches to 6 inches thick inside the vapor barrier (foil side facing the interior). Press it down to create a ¾-inch air space between it and the interior wall. Cover the interior wall with either tongue-and-groove or shiplap paneling.

STEP 5
INSULATING THE ROOF

A sauna roof must be built very tight to retain heat and keep water out. Ask a local contractor how much pitch the roof should have for snow conditions in your area. An eave of 1 foot or so is recommended for runoff. The roof should be sheathed in roofing plywood, covered with a layer of felt strips running horizontally, and covered with over-

CONSTRUCTING THE FLOOR

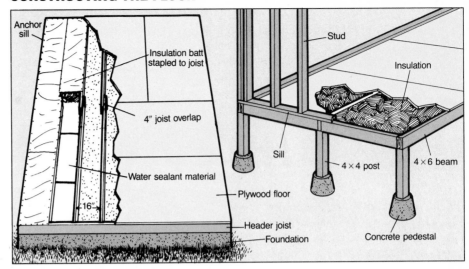

Since the floor is the coolest spot in a sauna, almost any material will work. Be sure it's well insulated in any case.

INSULATING THE WALLS

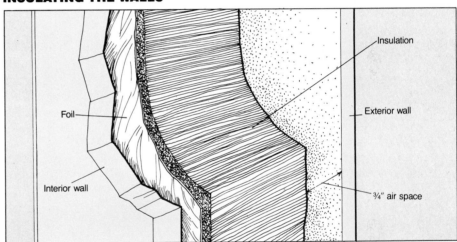

Free-standing outdoor saunas need a layer of aluminum foil inside both the insulation and the exterior paneling to create a vapor barrier.

INSULATING THE ROOF

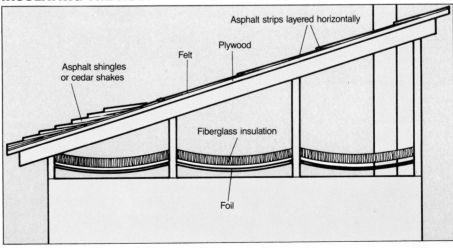

The roof is the crucial factor for retaining heat. Use aluminum foil and foil-backed insulation batts for a tight seal.

lapping shingles. Although wooden shingles may look more rustic, they are not as water-resistant as asphalt. The entire roofing construction must be perfectly tight to prevent heat loss. Beneath the roof apply insulation, leaving an air space in the attic area between the sauna ceiling and the batts of insulation.

STEP 6
MAKING A WINDOW

A sauna stoveroom is not meant to be brightly lit, so the windows, if there are any, ought to be rather small. But let size and placement be determined by your view and the direction of the sun. Watching a sunset in the evening or a view of the starlit sky enhances the sauna experience. Some saunas have stained glass or colored marbles dropped between double panes to create atmosphere. In fact, double panes of tempered glass will help retain heat and prevent steaming. Use a 1 × 2 to separate the two panes and quarter round and rubber caulking to seal them.

STEP 7
INSTALLING A WOOD-BURNING STOVE AND CHIMNEY

The romance of the sauna in an outdoor cottage almost cries out for a wood-burning stove. In spite of the inconvenience of stocking wood, cutting it, the extra time the stoveroom will take to heat up, and the need to stoke the fire and clean up afterward, many people enjoy the sensual mystique that only a wood-burning fire can provide. Your manufacturer will tell you how large a stove you need to heat your sauna.

Since a wood-burning stove is not as controllable as gas or electric heaters, fire is always a hazard and safety precautions must be rigorously enforced in both stove installation and use. Distance from flammable materials is the best fire prevention technique. Always place the stove at least 9 inches away from walls. Place fireproof wallboards

or cement strips behind the stove, extending beyond both sides of the stove by at least 1 foot. Block the boards or strips out from the wall with 2-inch furring to leave an air pocket between them and the interior wall paneling.

Never set a wood-burning stove directly on a wooden floor; use a stove pad. A simple brick foundation is easy to lay and usually complements the natural wood tones of the room. Cement or concrete blocks, however, are just as reliable. In a primitive-style sauna, a layer of gravel also makes an

INSTALLING A WINDOW

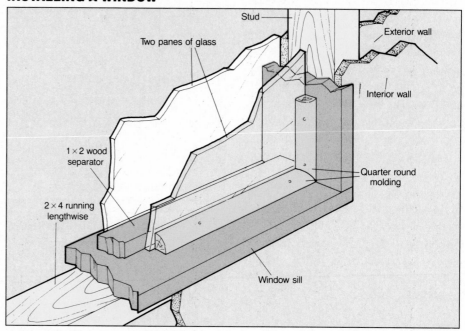

The easiest way to add a window is while you are framing the walls. Make the window frame a size that will fit between studs.

FIREPROOFING A SAUNA

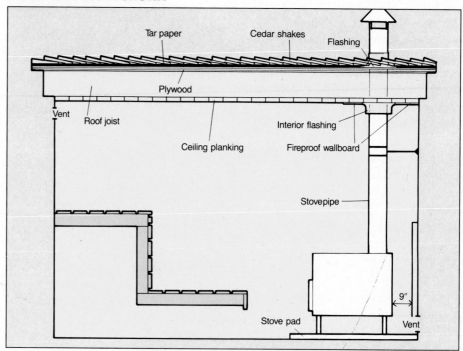

The extra care needed to make a sauna fireproof if you have a wood-burning stove is well worth it for the extra enjoyment it will bring.

efficient stove pad.

The chimney can go either out the roof or through the wall. In the latter case, the warmth radiating from the pipe can heat an adjoining dressing room or relaxation area. If the chimney exits through the roof, be sure to seal all the holes around it so they are watertight. Whether the chimney leaves through the ceiling or a wall, wrap fireproof tape around the pipe where it passes through other materials. Tin flashing is needed to cap the exit area. Finally, install chimney braces to secure the pipe away from the wall. Never let the chimney touch the wall.

STEP 8
PROVIDING A COOLING-OFF TANK

If your winter weather is not too severe, an outdoor cooling-off tank is a lot of fun. Guests feel liberated outdoors, the fresh air is stimulating, and splashing and dowsing can be a sociable respite from the hushed seriousness of the heated stoveroom. An old horse trough, a wooden rain barrel, a bathtub, even a garden hose will do the trick. A wooden barrel or trough can easily accommodate a garden hose adaptor installed through a hole drilled near the top. Fresh water running into the tub is always more inviting than the murky water typical of a tank after several uses. A spigot attached near the bottom makes for easy draining.

The tank area must have good drainage. Slope the ground away from the sauna itself so water will not run under the foundation. Split logs, walnut shells, or heavy gravel make a good ground cover around the tank. The point is to cover any dirt that will turn to mud and be tracked inside by bathers returning to the stoveroom.

The tank itself should be long enough and deep enough for an average-sized adult to submerge in completely. Ideally it should be large enough to hold several people at one time, either standing or squatting below water level. Cooling off between sessions in the stoveroom is meant to be a sociable and friendly experience, marked with camaraderie and good-natured frisking.

Locate the tank close enough to the stoveroom so that the distance doesn't discourage trips to it in cold weather. Also, ensure your guests' privacy around the tank with fences, shrubs, or other structures so they will not feel self-conscious about going outdoors nude. Good fences or windbreaks will make the trip to the tank more enjoyable on windy days or nights.

AN APRÈS-SAUNA COOLING TANK

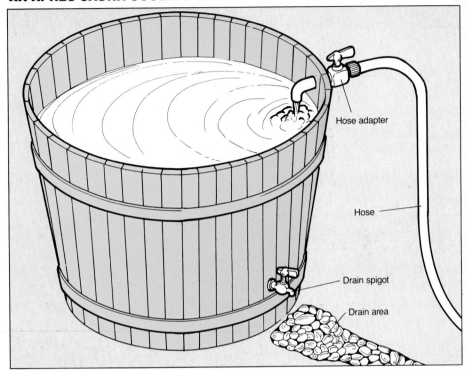

Almost any large container that will hold water and a human body can serve as a cooling-off tank outside the sauna.

THE COMPLETED OUTDOOR SAUNA PROJECT

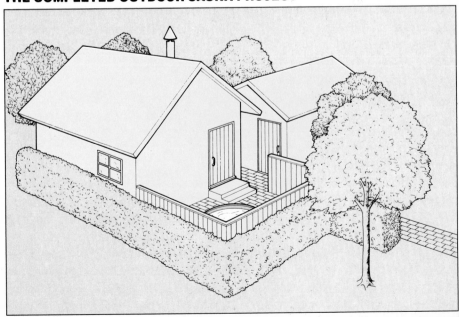

3 EXERCISE ROOMS

The human body thrives on activity, yet sedentary lifestyles prevent most of us from staying physically strong, flexible, and trim unless we make a special effort to exercise. For the past twenty years, people with a fitness fixation have relied on regular use of health club facilities to solve this dilemma. A whole new generation of fitness buffs, however, has come to appreciate the convenience and practicality of having a home exercise room, and manufacturers of exercise paraphernalia have been quick to respond with a wide range of products that are compact, versatile, effective, and relatively inexpensive.

There are several reasons why a home exercise room offers an ideal environment for staying in shape, whether it's used as a substitute for, or in conjunction with, a health club. A home exercise room saves the time spent traveling to and from a club, not to mention the time spent socializing and waiting in lines to use individual pieces of exercise equipment. It also enables you to exercise whenever you want. You don't have to schedule workouts around hours when your health club is open or less crowded, and you can exercise on days when inclement weather prevents outdoor exercise or even discourages you from going to your health club.

One of the biggest advantages of a home exercise room is that it gives you a powerful incentive to maintain an ongoing workout program. It's right there at home to remind you to exercise, and it can be furnished with equipment, accessories, and design elements that specifically suit your personal needs and desires. You can take advantage of spur-of-the-moment impulses to exercise; and you can incorporate fitness routines into other domestic routines, such as watching television, listening to music, supervising small children, cooking, or doing laundry. Above all, a home exercise room is a place that you can enjoy either by yourself or with family members and friends.

The ideal place for an exercise room is a little-used guest room or a bedroom vacated by a teenager who has left home. Of course, a large corner or alcove may be all you need. If you live in a house, check out basement, garage, or attic locations. In an apartment, you may want to convert a large closet or a wide hallway into exercise space. Be sure to consider what people may be doing in areas immediately above, below, or beside the exercise area. Activities like weightlifting, running on a treadmill, or punching a bag are apt to be noisy.

Whatever your ultimate plans for ex-

ercise space, the best procedure when you first decide to exercise in your home is to begin right away on a modest scale. A simple 6 × 2-foot mat and two pieces of equipment for your den, TV room, or bedroom will get you going. It's good to have more than one apparatus, though, so you don't get bored and give up. Use an inexpensive screen or folding wall to conceal the equipment or buy portable equipment that can be stored under the bed, in a chest, or in a closet. Taking this modest initial approach will help you to determine through experience exactly how you want to exercise at home and what you will need in terms of equipment and space design to realize your wishes.

Pleasant surroundings make exercising easier psychologically. Commercial health clubs use bright lights, garish colors, and fast-paced disco music to keep you moving so you won't create a bottleneck. But many people prefer subdued colors, peppy but not monotonous music, and modular lighting for different moods (for example, very dark for stretching; brighter for lifting weights). A good wall-sized mirror creates a larger-looking room and lets you observe your posture. After all, exercising is meant to be a narcissistic activity!

So many companies manufacture so many different kinds of exercise devices today that it is essential to shop around. There are more than seventy companies that produce stationary bikes alone and each has a half-dozen models. Chain stores and department stores offer the best bargains, but often the salespeople are not very knowledgeable. Sporting goods shops and specialty stores have a higher mark-up, but the clerks are usually rather well informed. So shop at the specialty stores and buy from a department or chain store or mail order catalogue.

Sometimes health clubs sell used equipment at very good prices when they replace it with newer models. The classified ads are another source for used equipment, since many people overbuy or lose interest in exercising. Wear loose clothes when you shop so that you can test the floor models. Floor models have already taken a good beating, so you should be able to tell from the condition of a given piece of equipment how well it holds up. Avoid lightweight metal or plastic frames and tubing with a narrow diameter. Chrome or paint that chips and parts that rattle should be a warning to you. You want equipment that is solid, durable, and long-lasting. It helps to read up on the latest technological designs and materials in the fitness magazines too, since innovations occur regularly.

Your first purchase should include an exercise mat for stretching, a set of free weights, a stationary bike for the legs, and a rowing machine for the arms, shoulders, and upper torso. With these four pieces of equipment you can begin a fairly comprehensive program and add other items as you go along. Single-purpose machines are great for exercising and strengthening one part of the body, but they are meant to be used with others that collectively cover all the parts of the body. You most likely don't have the space or money for a complete set. But if you have been plagued all your life by some weak area, such as your lower back or legs, you might want to buy an exercise device made especially to develop that part or to avoid straining it.

INDOOR EXERCISE ROOM COMPONENTS

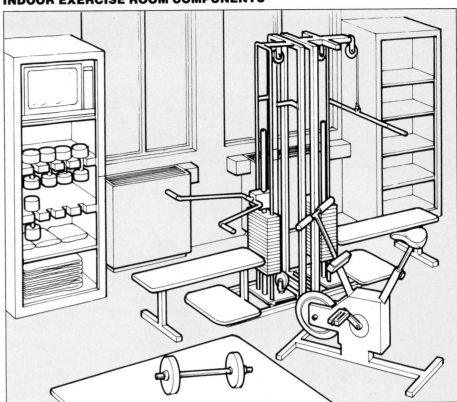

A classic indoor exercise room efficiently provides space for stretching, aerobic exercise on a stationary cycle, and weightlifting with free weights and a multigym. Note the custom-built cabinet for TV, weights, and towels.

OUTDOOR EXERCISE ROOM DESIGN

A luxurious exercise complex combines (from left to right) a dressing and relaxation room, a tiled spa and shower, and an exercise room, all of which open onto a deck and pool. A beautiful complex like this provides strong incentive to keep fit.

Equipment Types and Basics

The type of exercise equipment you buy depends on your personal preference as well as the limitations of your space and budget. Some fitness goals (such as those involving high muscle definition) are best achieved with a particular type of equipment; others (such as those involving muscle strength and flexibility) can be achieved with many different types of equipment.

FREE WEIGHTS

Free weights are the cheapest and simplest equipment with which to begin a home exercise program. With weights alone you can start an effective body-building program that can eventually be supplemented by more elaborate and expensive machinery. Unlike more complex multigym equipment, free weights take up little room and can be stored when not in use. They allow a wide range of movements and let you exercise just about all the major muscle groups.

An average set consists of a 5-foot bar weighing about 20 pounds, a set of weight plates, and two collars to secure the plates to the bar. The bar should have two knurled areas to provide a safe hand-grip area. The plates are round weights made of iron with a plastic coating or of solid dense rubber. Bare iron weights require thick carpeting or mats to work out on. Weights that come in 3- to 5-pound increments let you increase your total lift slowly as you build up strength. Begin with a modest set that totals 80 pounds and buy additional plates as you progress.

Your initial set should include an assortment of dumbbells for one-hand lifts. There are two popular versions: either the one-piece model made of metal or dense rubber or the dumbbell bar with removable plates.

The simplest weight bench is a solid one-piece structure for bench presses

BASIC EXERCISE EQUIPMENT

Free-weight assemblies usually include two 45-pound plates and four each of 25-, 10-, and 2½-pound plates.

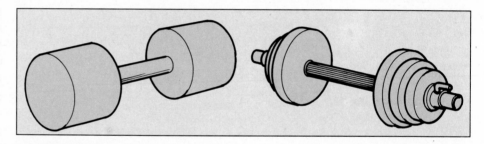

The dumbbell with removable plates can be adjusted to your needs. The solid-piece set includes 3-, 5-, and 10-pound weights.

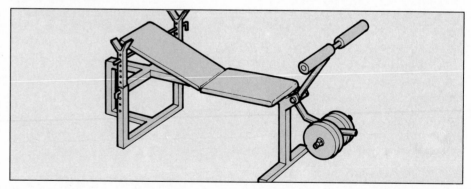

Incline weight benches can be adjusted to four or five different positions. Some weight racks telescope to vary the height.

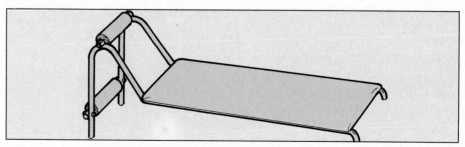

Test a slant board before you buy it for fit, for comfort in padding, and to make sure it will not wobble when in use.

performed lying flat on the back. An incline weight bench, however, can be adjusted to several positions. The varying slants put pressure on the torso at different angles so you work the muscles evenly.

A versatile model of the weight bench includes a leg curl/extension attachment bolted onto the front of the bench. You adjust the amount of weight by adding or removing the weight plates on the barbells.

Slant boards for sit-ups come in two styles. The one-angle board is fixed and cannot be adjusted. Other models allow several positions. Both are constructed to allow straight-leg and bent-leg sit-ups.

MULTIGYM MACHINERY

A multigym home fitness center can be as elaborate or simple as you wish. This first model includes a handlebar for bench presses, squats, leg presses, and chin-ups. The bar can be removed and replaced with leg and hand pulleys for leg pull-down exercises and arm pulls. Leg curl/extension bars at the foot of the bench can be attached to the weight stack with hooks. The bench itself can be inclined for sit-ups. A foot strap firmly secures your feet to the vertical beams. The original weight stack consists of eight 11-pound weights, to which additional ones can be added as you progress. When not in use the machine folds up and can be moved out of the way on its built-in caster wheels.

The second fitness training station is a bit more elaborate. The standard bench is used for chest and shoulder presses. The high pulley has an extension bar for working on the upper back and triceps. A low pulley can be fitted with handles or leg cuffs for doing arm curls or leg kicks. This piece of equipment comes with two weight stacks, a heavy one for the press station and a lighter stack for the pulley exercises. Variations on this model also provide leg curl/extension attachments.

The third compact machine includes the high and low pulleys, a press sta-

STANDARD EXERCISE MACHINES

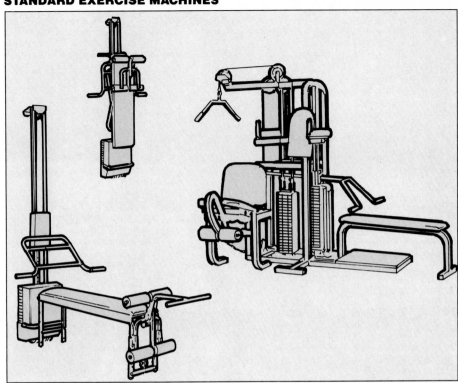

The one-person exercise machine (left) offers a variety of exercises for individual parts of the body. It folds up when not in use. The two-weight-stack model (right) lets two people work out at the same time. The bench is for leg curls.

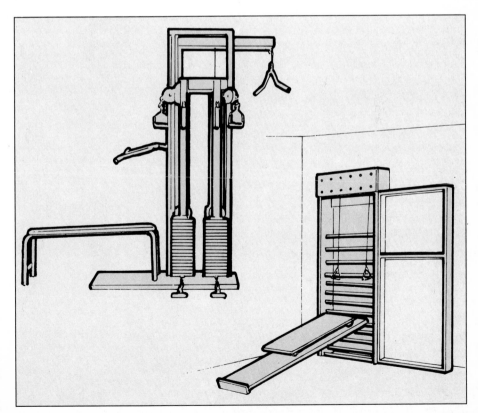

The two-weight-stack model at left lacks the leg curl station, but is more compact than the one shown above; it's a good buy for a small exercise room. Anyone handy with tools can build the model shown at right; it is attached to wall studs and offers six different exercise stations.

tion, and an incline bench. Like the preceding model, there are two weight stacks so that more than one person can work out at the same time.

The gym-on-a-wall can be built by do-it-yourselfers. For a nominal price you buy the plans, which include the building instructions and an exercise manual. You supply the lumber and parts. The slant board for sit-ups can be converted into a sliding bench that, with a system of pulleys, lets you use your own weight for resistance. Adjusting the bench at various angles increases tension. All the equipment conveniently folds up and disappears into the wall-mounted cabinet.

SPECIALIZED EXERCISE EQUIPMENT

A good stationary bike does not shake, rattle, or wobble. It must have adjustable resistance to increase tension as you grow stronger. A wide range of resistance that allows you to increase tension in small increments is best. Be sure the seat is comfortable and its height adjustable so you won't get cramped or saddle-sore. Don't buy a motorized bike. Muscle power, not electric power, must turn the pedals to achieve the aerobic effect.

An indoor treadmill will keep you in jogging shape during inclement weather. It builds stamina and endurance in addition to burning calories. The manual variety moves by your own jogging action while the motorized version proceeds at the pace you set on the dial. The electric treadmill moves in the direction opposite to the one in which you run. Keeping up with it is as strenuous as running on a manual model. Some treads can be inclined to simulate running uphill.

The rowing machine shown here has twin resistance cylinders; the oars slide back and forth on ball bearings. Select a model whose seat has several inches of thick padding so you aren't tempted to shorten your exercise period because of discomfort. Some machines have both a timer and a stroke counter. The simple one-piece handles move

only forward and backward, but more expensive models have the oars seated in swivels so that they can pivot. When using this type your arms pass through complete circular movements,

SPECIALIZED EXERCISE EQUIPMENT

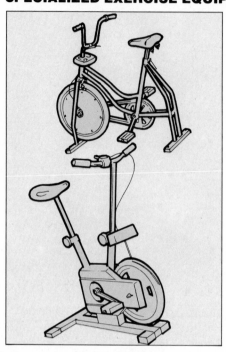
A good stationary bike has resistance controls on the handlebars so you can adjust tension without stopping the pedals.

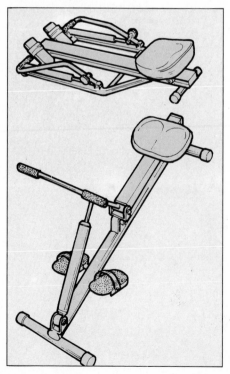
Some rowers have seats as much as 12 inches above the floor, which some people find more comfortable than lower seats.

thus stretching shoulder and back muscles to the maximum.

Indoor skiing machines are much gentler on the bones and joints than treadmills. The poling action exercises

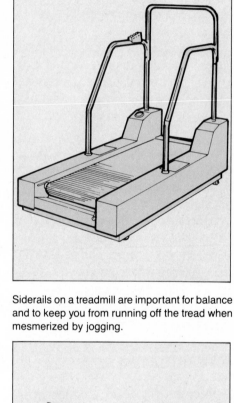
Siderails on a treadmill are important for balance and to keep you from running off the tread when mesmerized by jogging.

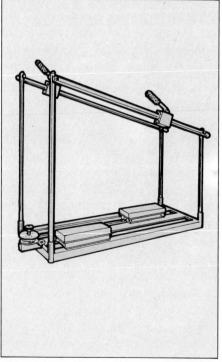
This unusual ski machine has roller-action handles on sloped side rails, thick cushions so you can exercise in bare feet, and adjustable resistance.

the shoulders, arms, and upper torso, which get no real workout jogging. All models have sliding foot pieces and either long cords with handles that move back and forth or hand-grips that slide up and down two parallel rails, as shown opposite. This model, only 5 inches high with the side rails removed, can be stored under a bed.

OTHER ACCESSORIES

Trampolines provide playful and enjoyable aerobic exercise, sometimes called "aerobic rebounding." Since trampoline exercise doesn't jar the bones and joints as severely as jogging or jumping rope, many people report fewer stress injuries using them. Many indoor models are small enough to store in a closet. Some fold up to save even more space. Indoor trampolines, like the larger ones for outdoor use, come in round and square shapes, which do not affect performance. A mat made of polypropylene is far superior to those made of nylon. Be sure that your floor can withstand the jumping and that your ceiling, of course, is high enough.

Chin-up bars are important exercise equipment. Even those who do not enjoy chinning can simply hang to let the spine and legs stretch out and relax. The doorway model is popular, as it can be installed in almost any doorframe and be removed when not in use. A more permanent model is made of rolled steel welded to wide plates that are spaced 32 inches apart so they will line up easily with wall studs. If this model is installed securely it can also be used with inversion equipment.

Inversion boots have become popular recently among health enthusiasts who seek to outwit the law of gravity. Inversion exercise is based on the principle that it is beneficial to let the organs, vertebrae, muscles, and even skin have a break from the unrelenting stress caused by the downward pull of gravity. It's also restful and relaxing once you get the hang of it. Some people enjoy doing twists, sit-ups, even working with weights in the inverted

position. A simple inversion bar securely mounted in a doorway and the boots and toggle bar are all you need.

A twist stand consists of revolving rubber pads that move on ball bearings as you twist the lower part of your body while holding onto the grab bar. Twisting tones the leg muscles, firms up the waist, and stimulates the cardiovascular system.

EXERCISE EQUIPMENT (CONTINUED)

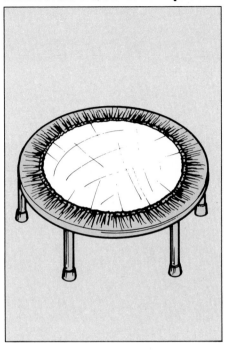

This round mini-trampoline has a rigid 1-inch-square tubing frame. The steel legs screw in. The skirt covers the springs.

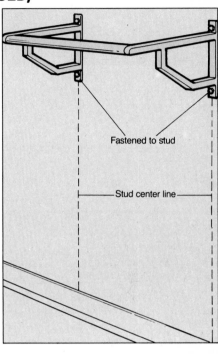

Fastened to stud

Stud center line

A reliable chin-up bar should be made from rolled steel welded to 3/16-inch-thick plates at least 2 inches wide.

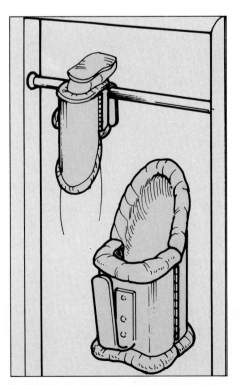

High-quality inversion boots are of heavy-gauge steel. Extra foam padding can be added for people with small ankles.

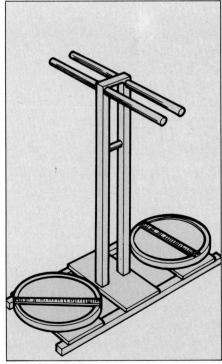

This dual twist stand provides back and hip exercise for two. Start stretching gradually so you don't pull a muscle.

Designing a Home Exercise Room

A home exercise room can be as elaborate or as simple as you choose. Exercise equipment can be kept in a bedroom closet and pulled out only when you use it, or you can redesign an entire room for the sole purpose of working out. Use pages 127 and 128 to construct a layout pattern to help you estimate how well your current furnishings and space will accommodate average-sized home exercise equipment.

Photocopy the templates of furnishings, equipment, and accessories (page 127) onto one sheet of paper and the grid (page 128) onto another. Then cut out the individual scale-sized templates on the photocopied sheet. Next, draw on the photocopied grid the dimensions of the room you intend to use for exercising. Let one square equal one foot. You are now ready to make your layout.

Place any templates representing existing furniture and equipment in their appropriate positions on the grid. Then play with the templates representing other exercise equipment and accessories, trying them in different positions to see how well they will fit. You might find that rearranging some current furniture or equipment will make better use of space. Keep in mind that some exercises require fully extended movements of arms and legs; allow enough room around you to prevent knocking or hitting anything. The sections that follow offer specific guidelines for designing an exercise room.

FLOOR
The floor must be solid and well supported if you plan to install heavy exercise equipment. Multigym pieces and a set of free weights will add several hundred pounds to the floor load. Determine in advance whether the floor can bear the extra weight. It's best to lay down a heavy mat or carpet in the area where you will exercise to make it easier on the feet and to muffle noise. If you buy carpeting, be sure to choose a style that is easy to clean and odor-resistant. Color-coding by paint, carpet, or mat can create aesthetically pleasing divisions between different exercise areas, such as aerobic and isometric areas.

CEILING
A room with a low ceiling may not be suitable for trampoline work or rope jumping. Certain types of equipment, such as rings, may have to be hung from the ceiling, so be sure you identify joist locations. If the room above the exercise room is used for quiet activities, such as sleeping or reading, you may want to drop the ceiling to allow space to install acoustical insulation. Also, think about what hangs on the ceiling directly above areas where you will be looking upward while exercising, for example, during bench presses or stretches. You don't want to wind up staring into a light fixture.

CONCEALED EXERCISE EQUIPMENT

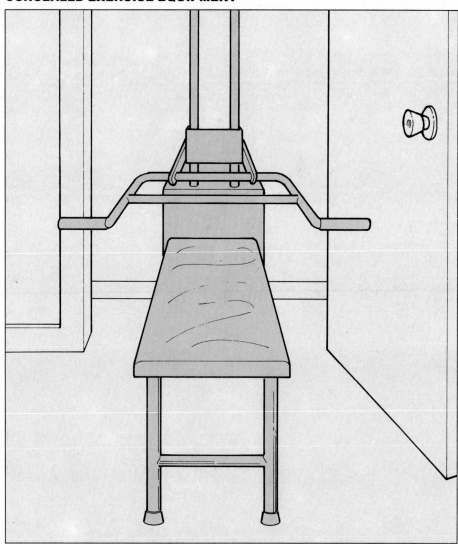

Where space is limited, compact exercise equipment can appear or disappear at will in any room of the house. Here, a weight-lifting machine folds out of a closet for easy access.

LIGHTING

Exercising doesn't have to be performed in the harsh glare of bright fluorescent lights typical of most commercial health clubs. In fact, many people prefer subdued lighting because it is more restful. Even though exercising with equipment is strenuous, there is something relaxing about it as well. Adjustable lighting levels are the best option. If you have modular lighting on dimmer switches, for example, you can bring it up to read a magazine while you ride the stationary bike, or turn it down to avoid distractions while doing yoga or stretching exercises.

If your equipment is in a room normally used for other purposes, you can focus track lights on it to emphasize the exercise space when you work out. Then when you finish turn them off or down low so that the equipment seems to recede from view.

WALLS

At least one wall should have a full-length mirror. Not only will it make the room look larger, a psychological advantage if you have to exercise in a rather confined area, but it will also let you observe your posture and movements so you can make certain you are doing exercises properly. Seeing yourself during a workout always helps motivate you to keep in shape, whether you are inspired by the progress you have made or the progress you need to make.

If you want to install a wall-mounted exercise device, the wall in that area must be strong enough to support it. It may be necessary to reinforce the wall studs.

Note window locations and arrange equipment according to whether you want an outside view while exercising.

VENTILATION

It's important to have fresh air while exercising. Since working out increases the rate of breathing, you'll be taking in more air than normally. So plan your exercise area in a room with a window that you can crack while exer-

A COMBINATION FOR EXERCISE AND RELAXATION

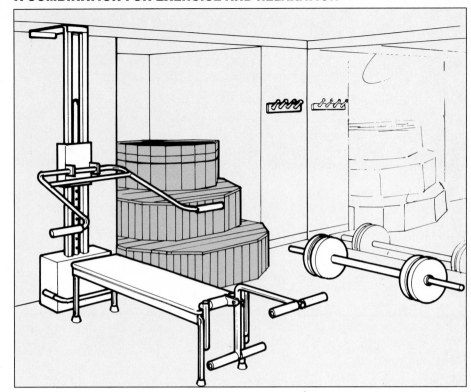

The centerpiece of this well-equipped exercise room is a hot tub, an ever-visible promise to the weary exerciser of a soothing reward for a strenuous workout.

A BASIC BUT EYE-CATCHING ENVIRONMENT

This small, simple exercise room is brightened by a full-length mirror and a large window that opens onto an attractive vista.

cising to ensure a rich supply of oxygen to the bloodstream. If you work out in a basement or attic without a window, use a fan to keep the air circulating. Aim it along a wall rather than directly on you. Health experts claim that the human body exercises best when the room temperature is about 70–72 degrees Fahrenheit. If it's too warm you may become overheated; if it's too chilly your body will have trouble loosening up.

COLOR

Paint the room a color that fits your concept of health and exercise. It might be a bright, energetic color or something more relaxing. The point is to make the room pleasant and motivating. Health or physical fitness posters on the wall may help; so might exciting graphics.

Graphics can also serve to create different exercise zones, as can different colors and textures in overall wall treatment. Be sure that wall paints and wall coverings are durable and easy to clean, since sweaty bodies can easily leave stains.

ENTERTAINMENT

Upbeat rhythmic music can set the mood for exercising and ward off boredom. You may want a tape deck, a record or CD player, one or two pairs of stereo speakers, or a radio as part of the equipment in the room. Some people enjoy listening to, if not watching, television and time their exercise sessions to their favorite programs.

Think about where the sound will be loudest (or the view best) in relation to where you will be performing different exercises. Also locate control switches and dials in convenient places.

A MULTI-PURPOSE LEISURE ROOM

This full-scale leisure room includes exercise equipment as well as a comfortable couch, a TV with large-screen projection, and sliding window-doors that lead to an outside patio.

A SPARTAN LAYOUT IN MODERN STYLE

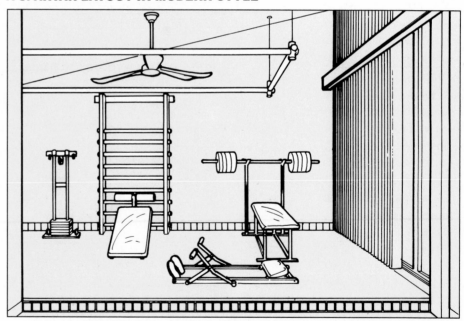

This crisp, uncluttered room concentrates the users' attention on exercise rather than on the surroundings. The only decorative element is the bare, chromed framework that surrounds the overhead fan.

Templates for Exercise Equipment

Make a photocopy of this page.

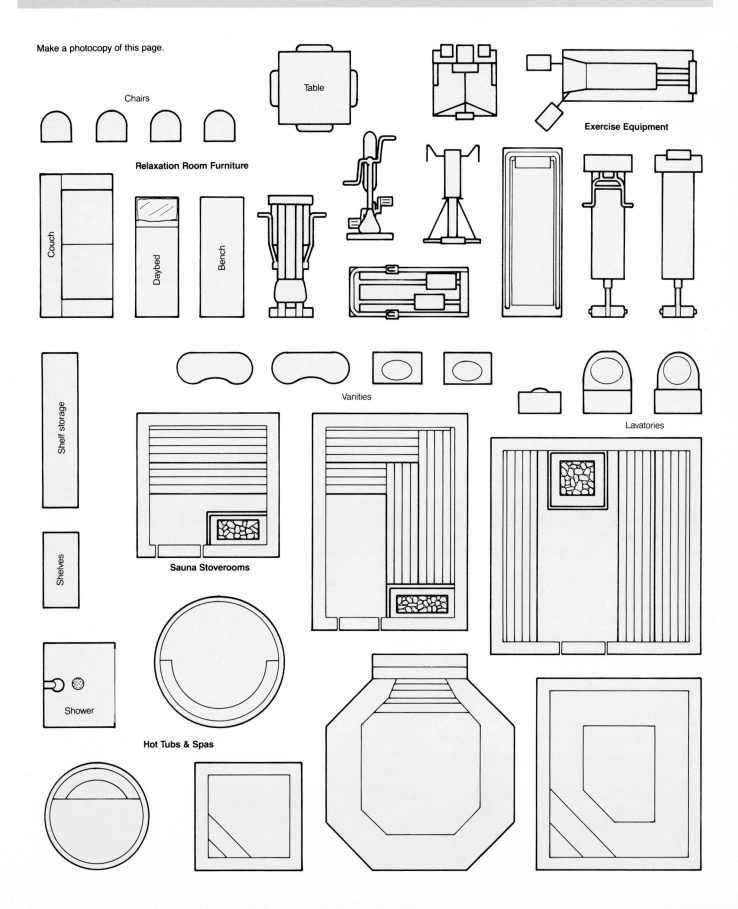

Chairs

Table

Exercise Equipment

Relaxation Room Furniture

Couch

Daybed

Bench

Shelf storage

Vanities

Lavatories

Shelves

Sauna Stoverooms

Shower

Hot Tubs & Spas

Planning Grid

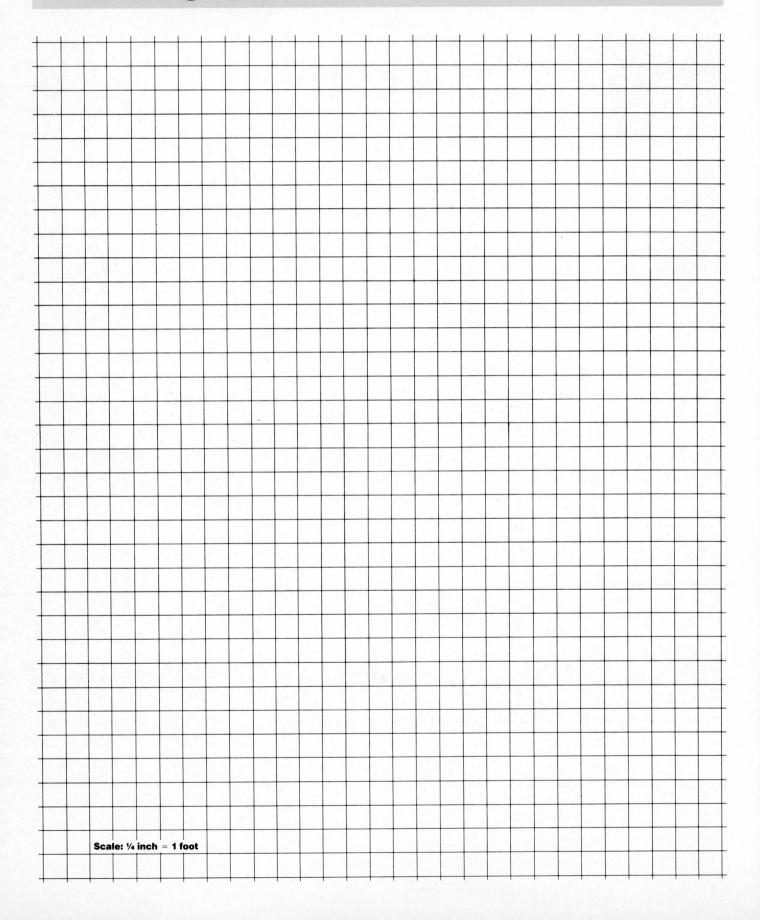

Scale: ¼ inch = 1 foot

The octagonal shape of this hot tub complements the angled platforms and steps of the surrounding deck.

Decks lead down to this covered hot tub, which offers a view of the broad, verdant valley below.

A prefabricated barrel sauna requires minimum outdoor installation labor. Bright flowers in planters that repeat the sauna's barrel design brighten the entrance.

A functional sauna can be worked into any odd corner of a house, as this design confirms.

This precut sauna for indoor installation takes up no more room than the average closet.

This prefabricated sauna makes use of one corner of an unfinished basement; later remodeling need not disturb the sauna.

This precut sauna features full-length thermal glass panels, an alternative to the traditional small, square window.

By incorporating this prefabricated sauna into the bathroom design, the architect provided for easier installation as well as homeowner convenience.

This sauna, part of the expansive complex shown at right, is a full-sized, carpeted room, with an adjoining *aprés*-sauna refreshment area.

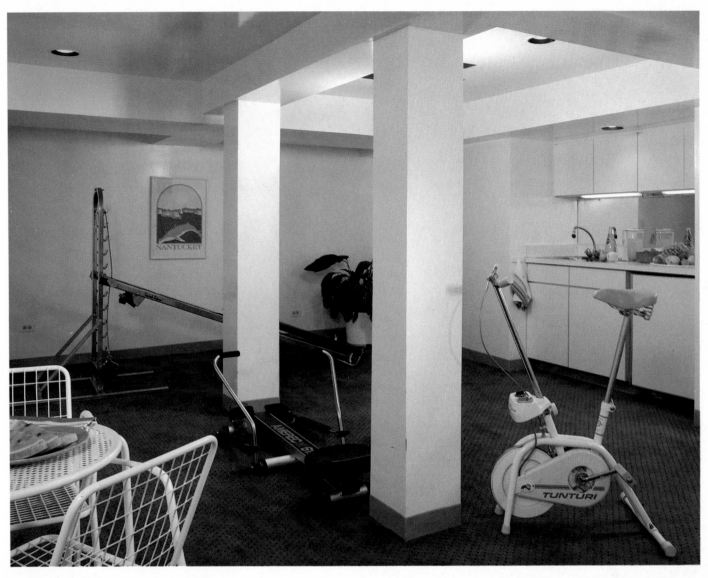

Adjacent to the sauna is an exercise area, which
houses just the right equipment for keeping fit.

A view from the ledge of the spa takes in this total
exercise and relaxation facility, a complex that
includes spa and sauna in a tiled area, plus exercise equipment, TV, and a wet bar.

This well-equipped exercise room includes two weight-lifting benches, trampoline, barre, and cycle, as well as closets and an antique wood stove.

Tucked into a basement corner, this exercise room is kept free of clutter yet manages to make room for the equipment essential to a thorough workout.

An interior exercise room can be brightened up with adequate lighting, light wall covering, and a mirror; a few thoughtfully placed lithographs and plants provide dashes of color.

Along with serious workout equipment, this room offers such creature comforts as an overstuffed divan, 'flagstone' carpeting, and multicolored lighting.

This high-rise apartment exercise room boasts clean, high-tech design; the full wall mirror seems to double the narrow space.

Monochrome surroundings, indirect lighting, and plenty of open space create a sense of peaceful calm in this urban exercise room.

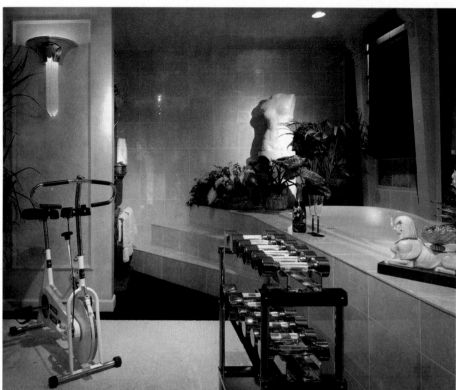

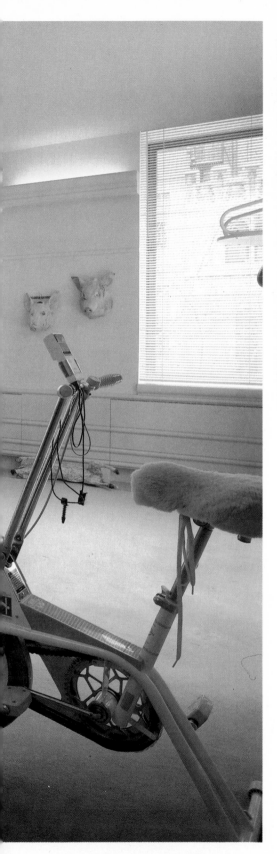

An air of classic elegance pervades this spa and exercise room; dramatic lighting heightens the effect of sculpture and gold-toned hardware.

Designed as much for relaxation as for exercise, this room—with its bright textile patterns and paintings—makes working out an attractive prospect.

For those who prefer a dramatic setting for exercise, this room uses low-level lighting with a few spotlights accenting the equipment.

4 WATER CARE FOR SPAS & HOT TUBS

A hot tub or spa should provide pleasure, relaxation, and physical well-being for its users. To ensure the peace of mind that enhances your total enjoyment of the benefits of thermal bathing, you'll want to know that the water is clean and uncontaminated. It should be free from health-threatening bacteria and germs and the dangerous minerals that can eat the wood of a hot tub, corrode the finish of a spa shell, or damage the support equipment. No matter what kind of hot tub or spa installation you have, you must conduct water maintenance on a regular basis, using the best possible equipment you can afford.

Maintaining clean water in a hot tub or spa is trickier than maintaining clean water in a large, unheated swimming pool. Because of the higher heat and the more confined area, tub and spa water can change more quickly than pool water. Even though there is much less water in a hot tub or spa than in a swimming pool, the impact of three or four people in the tub or spa is proportional to the impact of several *hundred* people in a medium-sized swimming pool. Such an overcrowded condition generates large amounts of water contaminants such as body oil, dirt, hair, perspiration, and personal grooming products.

High water temperatures create perfect breeding grounds for bacteria and algae that can quickly pollute the water. Heat also escalates the breakdown of the disinfectants you add to kill these bacteria and algae. In addition to the heat-caused problems in tub or spa water, there is the problem of accelerated evaporation. The swiftly aerated water coming through the blowers evaporates much more rapidly than the relatively placid water in a swimming pool. This process of speedy evaporation concentrates minerals that harden the water and damage the overall tub or spa system. As the *Spa and Sauna Trade Journal* put it, if you neglect proper maintenance, you'll have "a life-size petri dish of viruses, bacteria, algae, and gunk."

Proper maintenance for your situation depends on how often you use your tub or spa and the number of people who regularly bathe in it. Another factor to take into account is that the chemical composition of water varies from place to place, and the natural condition of the water you use influences your particular water treatment needs. Every spa owner has to devise a daily program of water maintenance that is based on both local conditions and on volume and frequency of system use. In general, two goals must be met: water must be sanitized to remove bacteria and germs, and in order for the sanitizing agent to function effectively, the water must be balanced between acidity and alkalinity.

A complete water-maintenance test kit provides all the equipment and instructions you need for testing the sanitizing power and chemical balance of your tub or spa water. The kit should include the means to take readings to measure free chlorine/bromine disinfectant levels, pH levels, total alkalinity, and calcium hardness. A DPD kit tests all four of these conditions. The OTO kits measure only total chlorine and pH.

You can install self-controlled chemical feeders that add the necessary chemicals to the water automatically when a sensor registers a low level. Since these are expensive, most people prefer to hand feed chemicals into their tubs and spas after making the necessary tests. A third type, the so-called robot feeder, adds chemicals at a fixed rate whether they are needed or not. Since robots do not sense which chemicals the water needs, they cannot guarantee that chemical levels are appropriate.

In addition to following a regular chemical maintenance program and testing regularly, you should let your filter run 2 to 3 hours each day, regardless of whether the tub or spa is used. After each use, let the filter run an additional 1 to 2 hours and chlorinate the water. A good filter running 2 to 3 hours each day will remove impurities as quickly as possible and help ensure that you have safe, clean water.

TESTING FOR PH LEVELS

The term *pH* refers to potential hydrogen in the water. Measuring the pH gives an indication of the relative acidity or alkalinity. Readings are expressed on a scale of 0 to 14. A reading of 0 to 7 is acidic; 7 to 14 is alkaline. The ideal range for a heated tub or spa is roughly neutral—from 6.8 to 7.6, depending on water temperature (see chart on page 148). Within this range, chlorine is most effective in cleaning the water without causing any bad side effects to the tub or spa components or, most important, to the bathers.

A reading over 7.6 is too alkaline, a condition that reduces the power of the disinfectant to prevent algae and bacteria growth. It also allows mineral concentration to build up and clog the filter. If left too long in this condition, the water gets cloudy and feels dirty, even gritty, on users' skin.

A reading of less than 6.8 is too acidic. Water with a high acid content corrodes metal in the plumbing system, eats the wood of a tub, and mars the finish on a spa. Eventually, it may even irritate the skin and burn the eyes of bathers.

You can correct the water pH level by adding soda ash (sodium carbonate) to raise alkalinity or by adding sodium bisulfate, an acid, to lower alkalinity. When adding an acid such as sodium bisulfate, carefully pour a dilute solution into perfectly still water so that it does not splash. If it hits you, it may sear your skin; and if you let too strong a concentration touch the sides of the tub or spa, it may cause surface damage. Muriatic acid, often used in swimming pools, is not recommended for tubs or spas because of the danger of making an overly strong concentration in such a small body of water.

To make a dilute solution of either of the two chemicals used to adjust pH, you'll need a one-gallon heavy plastic jug for each chemical, clear plastic measuring cups, plastic tablespoons, and a plastic funnel. Always read the

EQUIPMENT FOR WATER CARE

The basic tools you need for making dilute chemical solutions include 1-gallon plastic jugs, assorted measuring cups and spoons, and a plastic funnel.

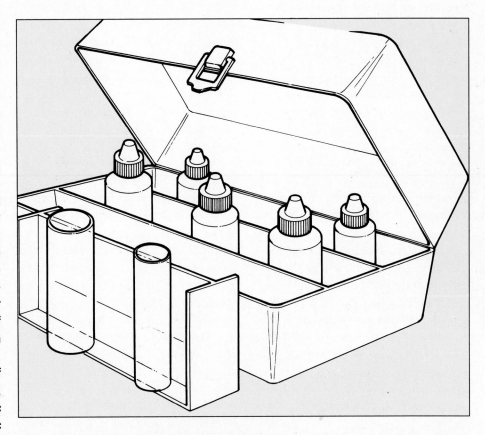

Water-testing kits come in many different forms, but all models include gauges and sample bottles for testing pH levels, calcium levels, and chlorine levels.

manufacturer's instructions when diluting chemicals, since the proportions can vary from one product to another.

MAKING CHEMICAL SOLUTIONS

Follow these processes when making chemical solutions to treat hot tub or spa water.

1. Begin by adding to the jug 2 quarts of water at room temperature.

2. Then pour in 2 cups of dry sodium carbonate or sodium bisulfate.

3. Mix until the chemical is well dissolved.

4. Then fill the jug with water. Never put the chemicals into the jug first, especially the acid. Always add them to water already inside the jug.

5. Consult the chart that is included in your manufacturer's instructions to determine the proper amount of dilute solution to add to our tub or spa water.

6. Add the appropriate amount of solution to the tub or spa water, following the directions given below.

TOTAL ALKALINITY

Your hot tub or spa water treatment program should include monthly testing for total alkalinity. This test indicates the amount of all the alkaline salts in the water. Some members of the alkaline family are necessary for well-balanced water. Other alkalines, especially those in carbonate form, can cause scaling and cloudy residue. The recommended alkalinity level is between 90 and 150 parts per million (commonly abbreviated to ppm).

Total alkalinity in tub or spa water is adjusted like pH levels. Add sodium carbonate to raise total alkalinity and sodium bisulfate to lower it. The same dilute solution used for pH levels will suffice.

ADDING DILUTE SODIUM CARBONATE SOLUTION

When adding sodium carbonate, follow this basic procedure:

1. Turn the circulatory system on.

2. Add the correct amount of dilute solution to the tub or spa water, pouring

WATER MAINTENANCE CHARTS

RAISING pH LEVEL WITH DILUTE SODA ASH SOLUTION

Gallons in Spa	Amount of Dilute Solution (see text) to Raise pH Level
100 gals.	add 2 Tablespoons
200 gals.	add ¼ Cup
300 gals.	add ¼ Cup + 2 Tablespoons
400 gals.	add ½ Cup
500 gals.	add ½ Cup + 2 Tablespoons
600 gals.	add ¾ Cup
700 gals.	add ¾ Cup + 2 Tablespoons
800 gals.	add 1 Cup
900 gals.	add 1 Cup + 2 Tablespoons
1,000 gals.	add 1¼ Cups

LOWERING pH LEVEL WITH DILUTE ACID SOLUTION

Gallons in Spa	Amount of Dilute Solution (see text) to Lower pH Level
100 gals.	add 2 Tablespoons
200 gals.	add ¼ cup
300 gals.	add ¼ Cup + 2 Tablespoons
400 gals.	add ½ Cup
500 gals.	add ½ Cup + 2 Tablespoons
600 gals.	add ¾ Cup
700 gals.	add ¾ Cup + 2 Tablespoons
800 gals.	add 1 Cup
900 gals.	add 1 Cup + 2 Tablespoons
1,000 gals.	add 1¼ Cups

RAISING CALCIUM HARDNESS (CH) LEVEL WITH DILUTE CALCIUM CHLORIDE SOLUTION

Add this Amount of Dilute Solution:	Hot Tub or Spa Capacity				
	200 Gals.	400 Gals.	600 Gals.	800 Gals.	1,000 Gals.
	To Increase CH this Amount:				
¼ Cup	12ppm	6ppm	4ppm	3ppm	2ppm
½ Cup	24ppm	12ppm	8ppm	6ppm	5ppm
¾ Cup	36ppm	18ppm	12ppm	9ppm	7ppm
1 Cup	48ppm	24ppm	16ppm	12ppm	10ppm
1 Pint	96ppm	48ppm	32ppm	24ppm	19ppm
1 Quart	NO!	96ppm	64ppm	48ppm	39ppm
2 Quarts	NO!	NO!	NO!	96ppm	77ppm

it in slowly around the perimeter.

3. Allow the tub or spa water to circulate for 30 minutes.

4. Then check to see if the pH level needs adjusting.

ADDING DILUTE SODIUM BISULFATE SOLUTION

When adding sodium bisulfate, an acid, to your tub or spa water, the procedure varies slightly. Follow these basic steps:

1. Be sure the circulatory system is *off* to prevent splashing.

2. Pour the solution into a narrow area in the *center* of the tub or spa water, using a slow, circular motion.

3. Let the solution settle, and then turn the blower on for 30 minutes.

4. Before bathing, check the pH level again and adjust it if necessary.

SANITIZING THE WATER

Heated water in a hot tub or spa should be tested daily, regardless of whether it's been used, to determine how much free chlorine is present. Whenever chlorine is added, part of it is imme-

diately neutralized as it attacks microorganisms and bacteria that cause the growth of algae. The remaining chlorine that is not initially neutralized is called "free" chlorine—which means it is available in the water to fight additional microorganisms as they enter the water.

It is important that the free chlorine count remain about 2.0 ppm at all times if you want to be absolutely sure of maintaining healthy water in your heated tub or spa. A free chlorine reading of 1.0 to 2.0 ppm is considered sufficient by most manufacturers of tubs and spas. Never use a tub with a free chlorine level below 1.0 or you definitely risk infection.

If you are using your tub or spa for a long period of time, such as all afternoon and into the evening, check the chlorine level every half-hour or so to keep the free chlorine count at 2 ppm. A standard estimate is that 4 adults in a medium-sized, 90-degree-Fahrenheit hot tub use up 3 to 3½ ppm of chlorine in about 15 minutes.

There are three types of chlorine on

the market: trichlor, calcium hypochlorite, and sodium dichlor. Only the third type of chlorine, sodium dichlor, is recommended for tubs and spas. Because the liquid form of sodium dichlor dissipates too quickly at high temperatures, use only the dry form. Being a neutral chemical, sodium dichlor does not seriously affect the pH level in the tub or spa water.

Bromine is becoming increasingly popular as an alternative disinfectant to chlorine, especially in tubs and spas. It doesn't evaporate as quickly as chlorine. Its odor is not as obnoxious, and most people find it easier on the eyes. The most commonly used form is sodium bromine, and the procedure is the same as for sodium dichlor.

A regular water-sanitizing program for any spa or hot tub, regardless of size or frequency of use, should include these steps:

1. It is essential to test the water systematically, on a daily basis; add moderate amounts of chemical whenever the chlorine or bromine level is too low. Add enough to bring the reading up to

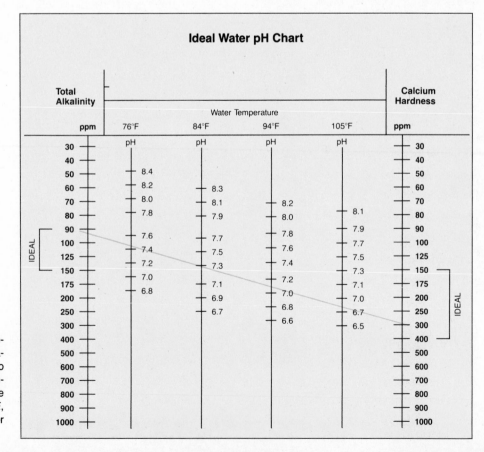

To use this chart, mark your alkalinity measurement on the scale at left and your calcium measurement at right. Draw a line between these two marks. Where this line crosses your water-temperature scale marks your ideal pH. On the above sample line, if your temperature is 94° F, the ideal pH is 7.1. Actual pH may be 0.2 above or below the ideal.

about 2.0 parts ppm.

2. After each bathing session, let the pump and filter run for 1 to 2 hours and chlorinate the water up to a free chlorine reading of 2 to 3 ppm.

3. Once a week, add enough chlorine or bromine to bring the count up to 10 ppm. This superchlorination, or "shock treatment," removes chloramines, substances chemically combined with chlorine.

In addition to these general procedures, always follow carefully the specific instructions on the label of the brand of chlorine or bromine you use.

CALCIUM LEVEL OR HARDNESS

Calcium is what makes water hard. Some calcium in hot tub or spa water is necessary in order to maintain the correct overall chemical balance and to prevent corrosion. The proper range is between 150 and 300 ppm. To raise the calcium count, add a dilute solution of calcium chloride.

The total mineral content of water varies widely in different parts of the country. If the water in your area is very hard, that is high in calcium, one way to keep the calcium level down in your tub or spa is to add a water softener that your tub or spa dealer sells. You can also keep the calcium level down by adding fresh water to the tub or spa after every session. Lots of water is lost through splashing and evaporation each time a tub or spa is used. Adding fresh water lowers the increased mineral concentration and the calcium count in particular.

Another method of reducing calcium is to drain the tub or spa when the count gets too high and then add new water. Some localities enforce legal restrictions on draining your tub or spa. It's best to drain your tub into a septic tank system or plumb it into a sewer. Tub or spa water should not be emptied into storm drains or directly into the yard since any used bath water is considered waste matter. Be very careful not to let tub or spa water drain into fish-bearing waterways, where it can have

MEASURING WATER PH LEVEL

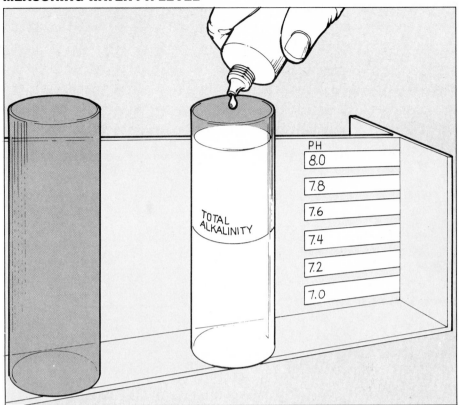

First, use your test kit to measure the pH level in your tub or spa water. Then check that level against the ideal level shown on the water chart on page 148.

MEASURING CHLORINE LEVEL

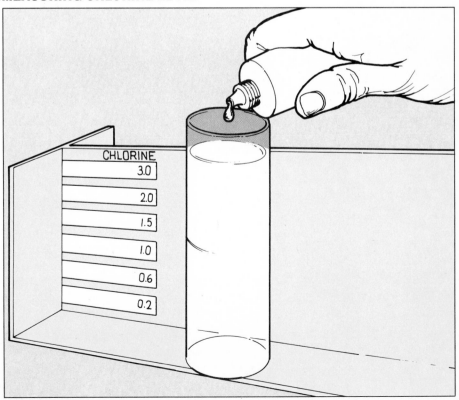

Measure the chlorine level in your tub or spa water with a test kit. A reading of 1.0 to 2.0 ppm is considered ideal.

an adverse effect on the fish, their food supply or, ultimately, their consumers.

BASIC WATER MAINTENANCE GUIDELINES

A complete water maintenance program for your tub or spa incorporates all the above considerations into a detailed and consistently followed routine. Record this routine on papers that are water-protected, so that they can be taken close to the tub or spa. One person should be responsible for all tasks to ensure that each task is performed on time and is not overlooked. Ideally, each regular user assumes responsibility for all maintenance tasks during a given period of time—say, a month or more, on a rotation schedule. This helps each regular user to become thoroughly familiar with all maintenance requirements.

Here are the basic procedures that must be completed in any total water maintenance program for a hot tub or spa:

● Test the water daily for pH level and chlorine/bromine count.

● Test the water for total alkalinity and calcium hardness at least once a month.

● Drain and refill the tub or spa every 3 months, cleaning the unit well each time.

● Cover the tub or spa when it is not in use to prevent evaporation, to reduce heat loss, and to keep the water clean.

● Clean the tub or spa filter about once a month.

● Remove debris from the skimmer after each use. The skimmer basket is a prime breeding area for bacteria.

● Remember that some of these tasks may need to be performed more often depending on the water volume of your installation, the frequency of use, the number of bathers who use your facility in a single session, and the general condition of the water and air in your locality.

● If any bather develops a rash after using your tub or spa, drain the tub as soon as possible before the next use and disinfect it with a dilute chlorine

AN ALTERNATE CHLORINE TEST

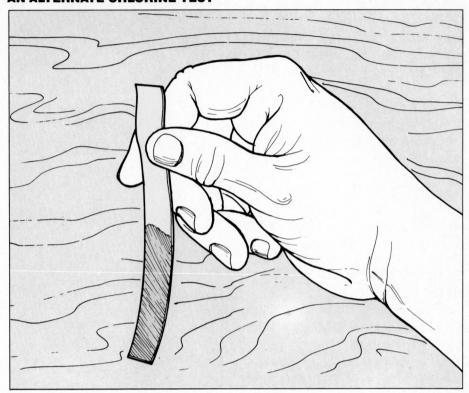

Test strips that change color are an easier, though less specific, method for checking the amount of free chlorine in your tub or spa water.

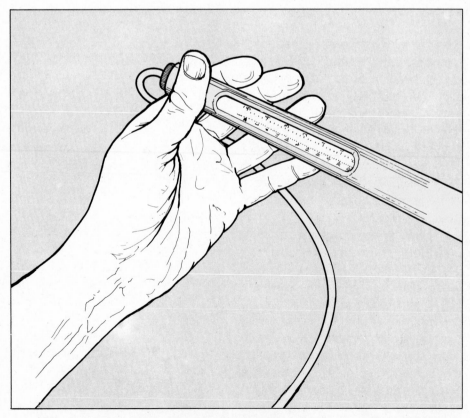

An accurate water thermometer is a vitally important tool in your tub or spa maintenance program. Check water temperature before adding any chemicals as well as before bathing.

solution of ¼ teaspoon of sodium dichlor to 5 gallons of water. Use rubber gloves and scrub all surfaces with long-handled brushes dipped in the solution. Do not inhale fumes or get the solution on your skin or in your eyes. If the bather's rash does not clear up in 7 to 10 days, report it to a doctor and to the local health department. (Some health departments test hot tub water samples for a fee. Call the lab of your local department to see if it provides this service. If it does, find out how to collect and handle sample water.)

SAFETY GUIDELINES

Remember these commonsense safety measures when using a hot tub or spa: find out from a doctor how thermal bathing may affect any personal health problems; avoid remaining in a hot tub too long (30 minutes maximum); enter and leave the tub or spa carefully to avoid slipping; always keep electrically operated devices at a distance from the water.

There are also important safety guidelines to follow while maintaining the water in your tub or spa. Chemicals can be very dangerous when they are not stored or used properly. Some can explode. Some can damage skin, wood, or fiberglass. Some can emit harmful gases. Some can do all these things. Many chemicals become unstable, and therefore possibly more dangerous, over a long period of time, or when exposed to a certain temperature, or when combined with moisture or other compounds. Read the warnings on the labels and in the instructions.

To ensure that your water maintenance program is safe for you, your equipment, and anyone who uses your tub or spa, always follow these safety habits:

● Make sure your maintenance program includes safety precautions.

● Make sure that young children stay away from the immediate vicinity while you are working with chemicals.

● Make sure you read the chemical manufacturer's instructions thoroughly

WATER TROUBLESHOOTING CHART

Problem	Quality Desired	Treatment
Colored or cloudy; foaming	Clean, clear, pale blue-green color; no foaming	Increase filtration time. Clean filter and filter equipment. Adjust pH and chlorine levels, if necessary.
Chlorine odor, foul smell; burning of eyes or skin	Clean, fresh odor	Remove chloramines with 10 ppm superchlorination. Test for free chlorine level. Adjust if necessary.
Hard (gritty) or slimy feel	Smooth feel	Check chlorine, alkalinity, and pH levels. Adjust if necessary. Increase filtration time.

and that you understand everything that is stated. If you do not, ask the manufacturer for clarification before you use the product.

● Follow all instructions exactly as they are written.

● Mix different chemicals together only if you are instructed to do so by the manufacturer. Even mixing two different brands of chlorine together may produce a violent reaction.

● Store all chemicals in a locked area that is cool and dry, and off-limits to children. Don't store them in an enclosed space that contains the support equipment, since some chemicals give off fumes that can corrode metal. Ideally, keep the chemicals near the tub or spa to prevent spillage or accidents while they are carried back and forth.

● When making dilute solutions, add the chemicals to water, *not* vice versa. This prevents unwanted splash-

ing or damage to the container.

● Do not add different chemicals to the tub or spa water at the same time. Allow at least 10 minutes between each chemical administration. Allow an hour between adding chlorine and acid.

● Always add chemicals in a dilute form unless instructed otherwise by the manufacturer.

● Be careful not to splash acids on skin, clothes, furnishings, or grass.

● Turn the pump off before adding chlorine or acid so that high concentrations won't get into the support equipment and corrode it. Run only the blowers to mix these chemicals in the water.

● Read the instructions carefully whenever you switch brands. Different brands may call for different concentrations.

● Always wash your hands thoroughly with soap and water after handling chemicals.

Hot Tub Maintenance

One of the great virtues of a hot tub, as opposed to a spa, is the warm, natural look and feel of the wood. The only disadvantage of wood is that, compared to plastic, it requires more conscientious care.

Wood is much more porous than the tough surfaces of fiberglass spas and therefore needs special treatment if you wish your hot tub to give you equally long-term bathing pleasure. Proper care of a wooden hot tub is not so much a matter of difficult or time-consuming labor as it is of consistent observation and attention. Normal, easy-to-perform maintenance procedures can keep hot tubs in most climates in peak condition for up to twenty years, at which time it may be necessary to rebuild with new wooden components; invisible inside-rot may have set in, even if you are unable to detect any evidence of decay or damage.

Specific guidelines for maintaining a tub vary slightly according to the type of wood used for the tub and the overall tub design, so your primary care reference source should be your dealer's and manufacturer's instructions. Be sure these instructions are written down, waterproofed, and readily available.

BASIC MAINTENANCE STEPS

Here are some important basic procedures for maintaining any wooden hot tub, regardless of the type of wood used in its construction or its overall design.

1. Never let the tub stand completely empty of water for more than 2 days, because without water the individual wooden staves will begin to shrink and the tub eventually loses its water-tightness.

If you live in a damp, relatively cool climate, such as the mid-Atlantic or Pacific Northwest United States, you can let a wooden tub stand only half-full of water during periods when it is not in use and no harm will result.

If you live in a hot, dry area, such as the southwestern United States, keep a wooden tub completely full of water all the time.

2. If the wooden staves of your hot tub are beginning to leak (look for dark spots spreading out from exterior seams that have not yet produced visible dripping), you can immediately prevent further damage by packing absorbant cotton twine into the outside joints.

Use a putty knife to push the twine into the joint between the two affected staves. Take care to pack the twine firmly, and the two staves should very soon swell back to normal, resealing the seam.

3. A leak between staves that produces visible dripping is a far more serious condition. It may be due to the staves not having been assembled properly. This is almost surely the case if there are several dripping leaks or several dark-spot leaks that do not clear up a week after being packed with twine.

This kind of serious leaking may necessitate tightening the hoops or even taking the entire tub apart and realigning the staves. You may possibly need an additional, custom-cut stave to fill in a sizable gap when the other staves have been tightly realigned. Discuss the situation with a knowledgeable dealer first, however, before taking any action.

STOPPING STAVE LEAKS

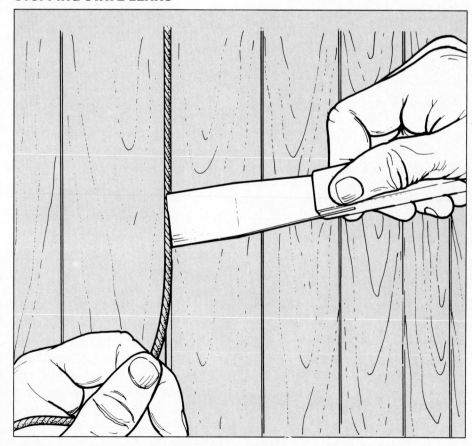

Force cotton twine between two hot tub staves with a putty knife to stop a leak and allow the staves to swell together again.

4. The exterior surface of the tub can quickly develop a ragged, patchy look, especially if it is exposed to a lot of sun, rain, or wind. You can preserve the exterior finish by rubbing generous amounts of Danish oil or a thinned linseed oil into the wood three or four times a year. Be sure to rub vigorously until the oil has been completely absorbed, that is, until it no longer feels wet when touched.

5. Don't forget to coat the stave hoops with a preservative oil or antirust paint to prevent rusting. Touch up the hoops once or twice a year in a dry climate, three or four times a year in a wet climate.

6. The interior of the wooden tub is best maintained by following a careful water maintenance program. Never apply sealers to the interior of the tub in an effort to make the staves watertight and waterproof. The wood's surface must be kept open so water can enter the fibers and keep the staves swollen.

To keep the wood clean and fresh, empty the tub completely every few months (more often if it is used regularly by two or more people at a time), and scrub it down vigorously with a scrub brush and a garden hose.

7. After you've used your hot tub for a couple of months or more, you may notice growths that look like fuzzy strands of white hair on the interior surface of the staves. These growths are caused by overchlorination, which breaks down the lignin, the substance that holds the wood cells together. Put a stop to this condition as soon as possible; check regularly to see if it is developing.

When you first notice the hairs, you can restore the affected area by draining the tub and sanding the wood with waterproof sandpaper. Severe conditions may need a 120-grit sandpaper followed by a finer grade to smooth the roughened surface. When you have finished sanding, rinse out the tub thoroughly so that the debris from the sanding does not get caught in the filtration system. Keep the chlorine level under control.

CAUSES OF CROZE LEAKS

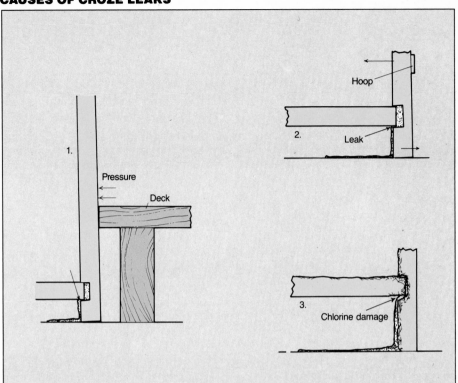

Hot tubs can leak at the croze if (1) the decking presses against the tub wall, (2) the lower hoop is out of alignment with the croze, or (3) the wood has been damaged by chlorine.

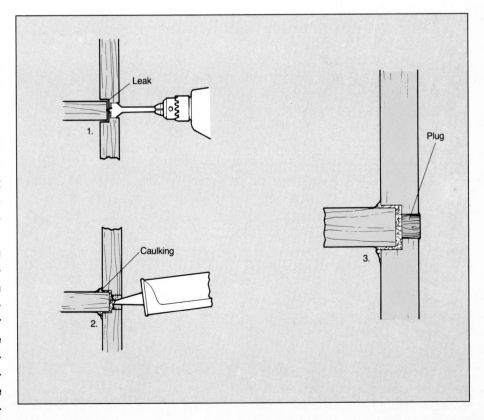

To repair a leak in the croze, (1) drill a hole completely through the stave from the opposite side; (2) inject silicone caulk to fill the gap; (3) close the hole with a wooden dowel plug.

Spa Maintenance

Fiberglass spas hold up rather well under normal conditions, no matter what the climate. They are specifically designed to be an improvement on the more vulnerable wooden hot tub—to be able to withstand more abuse and to be easier to clean. As a result, a spa will generally last far longer than a hot tub with far less effort on the part of the owner.

Nevertheless, environmental factors such as sunlight, wind, moisture, and dust, in addition to chemical mixtures in the hot water, all take their toll on a spa shell's highly polished surface. The color can fade and the polish can become noticeably marred through oxidation, abrasion, and corrosion. In extreme situations of neglect or abuse, the shell itself can sustain cracks and punctures.

Amino-functional sealants, the latest products in spa care, are designed to offer maximum protection to both the finish and the shell. These coatings bond chemically to the surface of the spa shell, unlike the wax-based coatings that merely spread over the surface and break down fairly rapidly.

The amino-functional fluids are composed of silica in a petroleum distillate base with a coupling agent. When the product is applied, the petroleum evaporates, leaving a hard crystalline shield that reflects the sun's heat and ultraviolet rays. This treatment can reduce color fading and oxidation by up to 90 percent. In addition, it leaves a high glossy finish. Not only is this finish very attractive, it is also virtually impervious to weather damage and helps prevent accidental scratching or piercing of the spa shell.

Since the amino-functional fluids bond completely to the shell itself, the shell surface needs to be as clean as possible before application. Be sure to remove any smudges, dirt, oil, and other chemicals with a spa-cleaning agent (available from your dealer) before applying amino-functional coatings, or you will wind up sealing these impurities into the surface.

Because spa shells are manufactured in a variety of ways using many different component combinations, you must follow your manufacturer's specific instructions for keeping up your particular spa. These instructions should be kept in written, preferably waterproof, form within easy access.

BASIC MAINTENANCE GUIDELINES

Here are some important basic guidelines that apply to all spas, regardless of individual variations in make or components:

1. The single most effective maintenance step for preserving your spa shell is to keep the interior spa water in proper pH balance (see page 145) and properly sanitized, which usually involves chlorination (see page 147).

It is especially critical to keep water soft, since calcium carbonates can rapidly eat away a fiberglass surface. Frequent draining of all spa water and the consistent use of a water softener will help ensure that the concentration of calcium carbonates does not have a chance to reach damaging levels.

2. Continually monitor the waterline for any signs of stain or algae. If you spot any stains or algae, remove them with a soft scrub-brush. Your spa dealer sells brushes that will not abrade the spa shell surface.

3. Whether or not you notice any

MAINTAINING SPA FINISH

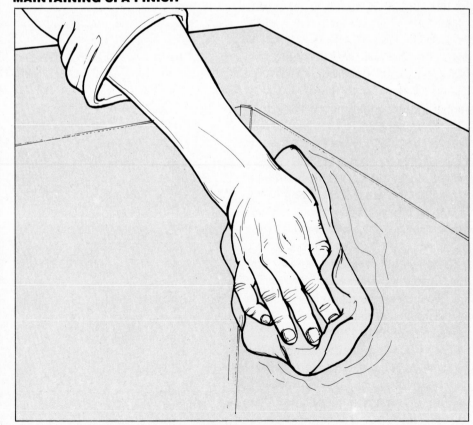

Amino-functional fluid provides a durable, shiny finish on the inside of a spa shell. Apply it as you would a wax every couple of months.

stains or algae in your spa shell, it's a good idea to give it a thorough cleaning on a regular basis, every couple of months in the case of normal use, and at least once a month in the case of heavy use.

First, drain the spa completely and brush off any dirt and algae that you can see. Then scrub down the entire spa vigorously with a nonabrasive cleanser (available from your spa dealer). Be sure to hose out the tub thoroughly before refilling it.

4. Use a weak solution of muriatic acid (about 1 part acid to 10 parts water) to clean the tile border if your spa has one. Clean this border at the same time as you clean the spa itself, so that you can hose off the tile and the spa when you are finished.

5. Whenever you notice that the interior finish is beginning to fade, apply a coat of an amino-functional sealant that has been recommended by your dealer.

Be sure you spread the sealant evenly across the entire spa surface, rather than concentrating on particularly discolored areas.

While amino-functional sealants last much longer than regular wax-based coatings, they will not hold up forever. Even if you do not notice interior fading, you should reapply sealant periodically according to your spa dealer's or manufacturer's recommendations.

6. If the gelcoat surface suffers minor damage, such as scratching or small holes, you can make the necessary repairs yourself. Serious gouging of the surface with damage to the fiberglass structure underneath, however, will have to be repaired by professional technicians.

SIMPLE REPAIR PROCEDURE

Here are the steps for making minor repairs:

1. Clean the area around the scratch or hole and remove any wax or oil from inside the scratch or hole itself.

2. Smooth the affected area with sandpaper or a burr attachment on a power drill. Feather the damaged

FILTERING TAP WATER

Untreated tap water can mar the finish of a gelcoat or acrylic spa surface. Cover the hose nozzle with a clean towel to filter the water before it enters the shell.

COVERS FOR SPAS AND TUBS

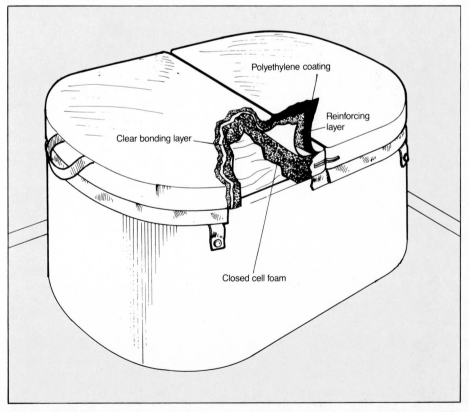

Foam-filled spa and hot tub covers act as thermal blankets, retaining heat, reducing evaporation, and preserving an optimum chemical balance more effectively than standard covers.

edges with sandpaper, smoothing out any roughness. You may have to sand first with a coarse-grained paper, and later with a finer-grained paper, so that the affected shell surface is not raspy to the touch.

3. To a small amount of colored gelcoat add 2 drops of catalyst, fiberglass filaments, and mix the substances thoroughly. This is best achieved by rapidly cutting or whipping the solution rather than merely stirring it.

4. Use a putty knife to fill the hole or scratch with the gelcoat-catalyst mixture to about 1/16 of an inch above the surrounding surface.

5. Lay a piece of cellophane gently over the patched area and allow it to partially cure for about 15 minutes.

6. Remove the cellophane when the underlying substance feels rubbery, and trim the patch slowly and carefully with a razor blade or small trowel so that it is exactly flush with the surrounding surface.

7. Drop a small amount of the gelcoat alone onto one edge of the patch, cover it with cellophane, and squeegee it with a single-edge razor blade until it is smoothed in with the surrounding area.

8. After 2 hours remove the cellophane and sand the area with moistened 600-grit sandpaper. Rub or buff the finish smooth with a rubbing compound. The patched area may look darker than the rest of the spa, but the color should weather until it matches the original.

REPAIRING SPA SURFACE DAMAGE

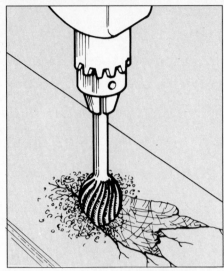

1. If the surface of a spa shell suffers minor damage, first roughen the affected area with a drill burr.

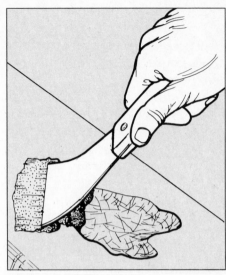

2. Using a putty knife, apply a mixture of gelcoat, short fiberglass filaments, and catalyst to the damaged area.

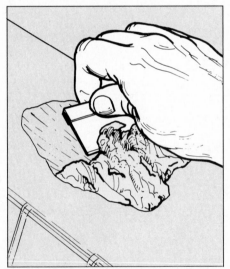

3. Place a square of cellophane over the patched area. When the mixture is partially dry, remove the cellophane and scrape the patch smooth with a knife or razor blade.

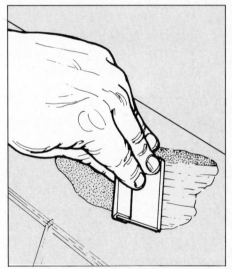

4. Apply gelcoat alone to the top of the patch, lay cellophane over it, and smooth it with a razor blade. When the patch is completely dry (1 to 2 hours), sand with fine-grained paper and buff it.

Glossary

Acrylic lining Hard plastic lining on the inner surface of a fiberglass spa.

Amino-functional sealant Protective silica coating for fiberglass spas that reflects ultraviolet and heat rays of sun.

Backfill Earth or other material used to fill excavated space around a spa or other construction in the ground.

Batter board Piece of lumber mounted horizontal and level on stakes as a support for the strings that guide the construction of forms for concrete.

Below-grade Lower than the normal level of the ground or other reference point.

BTU British Thermal Unit; a unit for measuring the heat produced by a stove or furnace; the amount of heat needed to raise the temperature of one pound of water 1° F.

Cartridge filter Common type of water filter used in the support system of a hot tub or spa that utilizes a replaceable or flushable container filled with plastic or paper purifying material.

Chime joist Heavy piece of lumber, e.g., a 4 × 4, placed horizontally to support the floorboards of a hot tub.

Cripple stud Short piece of framing (2 × 4) installed vertically to strengthen the wall framing around a doorway or other construction.

Croze Groove at the bottom of a hot tub stave into which the floorboard fits.

Curing In a sauna, the first heating and preparing of a sauna and its furnace or heater for regular use. Also, the chemical action that hardens concrete.

Dado joint See Croze

DE filter Diatomaceous earth filter; spa or hot tub filter that forces water through a very fine substance to trap residues, algae, and dirt.

Duckboard Wood walkway using narrow boards spaced apart to allow drainage.

Facenail To join one piece of wood to another by driving nails straight through the outer, facing surface.

Flash heater A type of spa or hot tub water heater that burns gas or oil in a large open flame surrounding a heat exchanger.

Footing Concrete or other firm support, at or in the ground, used as a base for the vertical posts of a hot tub, deck, etc.

Form Temporary construction of boards and supports into which concrete is poured; removed after concrete has cured.

Framing connector Metal device used to join two large framing members, for example, a post and a joist; the connector is nailed, clamped or otherwise securely fastened to each member, rather than fastening the members directly together.

Free chlorine Ions of chlorine gas in spa or hot tub water that are able to combine with and destroy impurities and microorganisms.

Free weights Individual exercise weights that are not part of a machine; for example, dumbbells.

Furring strip Thin, narrow strip of wood or metal attached to a wall or other surface to provide air space or support.

Gelcoat lining Polyester-resin lining on inner surface of fiberglass spa.

Gunite Fluid mixture of cement, sand, and water that is blown onto a reinforced base to construct a free-form spa.

Header joist Horizontal framing member placed above a door opening or other construction.

Heartwood Wood cut from the center of a tree; usually darker in color and longer-lasting.

Hose-bib fixture A valve installed in a pipe, which can be opened to drain the line.

Hydrojet Nozzle attached to the side of a spa or hot tub to create turbulence; also called venturi jet.

Hygrometer Device for measuring the relative humidity of the atmosphere.

Ionizer Electrical device that produces free ions for purifying air or water.

Inversion boot Boot with a hook by which the wearer is suspended upside down for exercise on a horizontal bar.

Leaching In a hot tub, the harmless process in which tannin washes out of the wood, discoloring the water.

Leg curl attachment Part of an exercise machine gripped by the legs for weight lifting or other exercise.

Muriatic acid Commercial name for hydrochloric acid; used as a cleaning agent.

On-center Point of reference when measuring; for example, "16 inches on-center" means "16 inches from the center of one stud to the center of the next."

Oakum and lead The old-fashioned materials used to pack and seal plumbing joints.

Ozone generator Device that produces ozone, O_3, an active purifying agent.

Penny (abbr. d) Measurement of nail size; for example, a 10d nail is three inches long; it takes 69 common 10d nails to make a pound.

pH Potential hydrogen; a measurement of the relative acidity or alkalinity of a liquid on a scale from 0 to 14; a reading of pH 7 is neutral.

Pier footing Raised block of concrete or stone that supports a pier; see Footing.

Placing concrete The process of pouring concrete into the forms, removing any air holes, and leveling it.

Plate In building construction, a horizontal framing member, for example, a 2 × 4, at the bottom or across the top of a wall.

Plumb *Adj.:* Vertical, straight, perfectly in line. *Verb:* To connect with pipes or tubes.

ppm Parts per million; a measurement of the concentration of a substance in a liquid; for example, water with 500 ppm of calcium is exceptionally hard.

Precut Parts of a construction, such as a sauna, that have been entirely cut to size and fit, but not assembled.

Prefabricated Parts of a construction, such as a sauna, that have been cut and assembled into large units, such as walls and ceilings, that are easily joined together by the buyer.

Prehung door A door that has been

mounted on hinges in a frame; this complete unit is installed by the buyer.

Preplumbed Joined together by all necessary pipes, tubes, and joints.

PVC Polyvinylchloride; a type of rigid plastic used to make pipe.

Quarter round Trim material for wood construction, with a right angle on one side and a ¼-circle opposite.

Return line Pipe that conducts clean water from the filter and heater back to the hot tub or spa.

Riser A board installed vertically between the stringers of a stair that supports the tread.

Robot feeder A device that adds chemicals to hot tub or spa water automatically.

Sand filter A filter that cleans spa or hot tub water by passing it through a container of sand.

Saunapala Food and drink taken for refreshment after a sauna to restore energy.

Shim A small piece of wood or other material installed between construction members, such as a door jamb and frame, to space and position them correctly.

Siphoning Drawing water back out of a spa or hot tub by unwanted suction in the return line.

Skid pack The mechanical and electrical devices needed to operate a spa or hot tub system, mounted together on a platform.

Skimmer A filter used to remove large debris, such as leaves, from hot tub or spa water.

Soda ash *See* Sodium carbonate.

Sodium bisulfate Chemical added to spa or hot tub water to increase the acidity.

Sodium carbonate Chemical added to spa or hot tub water to increase the alkalinity.

Solar heater Heater for spa or hot tub water operated by the sun's rays.

Spa shell The fiberglass bowl that holds the water.

Stave Vertical piece of wood that forms the sides of a hot tub.

Stoveroom The heated space of a sauna.

Stringer The diagonal board on the side of a stair that supports the treads and risers.

Stud Vertical framing member, commonly a 2 × 4, of a wall or other construction.

Suction line The water line that draws dirty water out of a hot tub or spa to the purifying equipment and pump.

Support system The mechanical and electrical devices necessary to supply, circulate, and purify hot tub or spa water.

Tank heater A hot tub or spa water heater in which a small flame heats a tank of water.

T-joint Three pieces of pipe or tubing joined in the shape of a T; a connector with three openings in the shape of a T.

Toenail To nail two pieces of wood together by driving nails at an angle through the edge of one piece into the other.

Tongue and groove A joint in paneling and floorboards, in which a narrow protrusion on one board edge fits into a narrow groove in the adjoining edge.

Tracer wire A metal wire laid alongside a buried plastic gas pipe so that one can locate the pipe with a metal detector.

Tread The horizontal boards in a stair, supported by the stringers.

Ultraviolet sterilizer An electrical device that generates ultraviolet rays used to purify spa or hot tub water.

Venn diagram A planning sketch that encloses main functional areas in a home or yard in circles or ovals.

Venturi jet *See* Hydrojet.

Vihtas A bundle of leafy branches used to strike the skin during a sauna bath to stimulate blood circulation.

Weight bench An exercise machine with a set of weights, usually adjustable, that can be lifted by arms or legs.

PHOTOGRAPHY CREDITS

Almost Heaven™ Hot Tubs, Ltd., 131

Arizona Custom Pools & Landscaping, 12 top, 59 bottom, 62 bottom, 63, 64 top, 66 top, 67 top

B & B Pool and Spa Center, installer, 51 bottom, 55 top, 56 bottom, 79

Barrel Builders, 78 top

California Redwood Association (George Lyons photo), 10

California Spa, 58 bottom, 59 top, 61 bottom, 64 bottom, 66 bottom, 67 bottom

Classic Pool & Patio, Indianapolis, 68, 69 bottom, 72 top, 73

Cording Landscape Design, Inc., Len DiTomaso, ASLA, 55, 75

Creative Energy, 74 bottom, 77 top

Creative Environments, 8 bottom

Jerry Demoney, photographer for Stockpile, Inc. and Ann Demoney, stylist, 15, 16, 50 bottom, 51, 52, 54, 55, 56 bottom, 60 bottom, 70, 71, 75, 78 bottom, 79, 132, 133, 134, 135, 138, 139

Dolphin Pool Supply & Service, 50 top, 69 top

Phillip H. Ennis Photography, 13, 140, 141, 142, 143, 144

Gerald Spa, 57 top

Hot Tubs International, 8 top, 12 bottom © Ron Jautz, 49

Michael Landis, 129

Peter Mauss/ESTO, 80 bottom

Mission Valley Pools & Spas, Inc., 58 top, 60 top, 61 top, 62 top, 65

National Spa & Pool Institute, 14 bottom, 53, 56 top, 57 bottom, 72 top, 74 top, 77 bottom, 80 top, 130

Perma-Built, 70, 71, 133

Sauna Factory, installer, 132, 134, 135

The Spa Shop, installer, 50 bottom, 52, 54 top & bottom, 78 bottom

Spas by Renée, 11, 72

Jessie Walker Photography, 2, 136, 137

Index

Metric Charts

LUMBER

Sizes: Metric cross-sections are so close to their nearest Imperial sizes, as noted below, that for most purposes they may be considered equivalents.

Lengths: Metric lengths are based on a 300mm module which is slightly shorter in length than an Imperial foot. It will therefore be important to check your requirements accurately to the nearest inch and consult the table below to find the metric length required.

Areas: The metric area is a square metre. Use the following conversion factors when converting from Imperial data: 100 sq. feet = 9.290 sq. metres.

METRIC SIZES SHOWN BESIDE NEAREST IMPERIAL EQUIVALENT

mm	Inches	mm	Inches
16 × 75	5/8 × 3	44 × 150	1 3/4 × 6
16 × 100	5/8 × 4	44 × 175	1 3/4 × 7
16 × 125	5/8 × 5	44 × 200	1 3/4 × 8
16 × 150	5/8 × 6	44 × 225	1 3/4 × 9
19 × 75	3/4 × 3	44 × 250	1 3/4 × 10
19 × 100	3/4 × 4	44 × 300	1 3/4 × 12
19 × 125	3/4 × 5	50 × 75	2 × 3
19 × 150	3/4 × 6	50 × 100	2 × 4
22 × 75	7/8 × 3	50 × 125	2 × 5
22 × 100	7/8 × 4	50 × 150	2 × 6
22 × 125	7/8 × 5	50 × 175	2 × 7
22 × 150	7/8 × 6	50 × 200	2 × 8
25 × 75	1 × 3	50 × 225	2 × 9
25 × 100	1 × 4	50 × 250	2 × 10
25 × 125	1 × 5	50 × 300	2 × 12
25 × 150	1 × 6	63 × 100	2 1/2 × 4
25 × 175	1 × 7	63 × 125	2 1/2 × 5
25 × 200	1 × 8	63 × 150	2 1/2 × 6
25 × 225	1 × 9	63 × 175	2 1/2 × 7
25 × 250	1 × 10	63 × 200	2 1/2 × 8
25 × 300	1 × 12	63 × 225	2 1/2 × 9
32 × 75	1 1/4 × 3	75 × 100	3 × 4
32 × 100	1 1/4 × 4	75 × 125	3 × 5
32 × 125	1 1/4 × 5	75 × 150	3 × 6
32 × 150	1 1/4 × 6	75 × 175	3 × 7
32 × 175	1 1/4 × 7	75 × 200	3 × 8
32 × 200	1 1/4 × 8	75 × 225	3 × 9
32 × 225	1 1/4 × 9	75 × 250	3 × 10
32 × 250	1 1/4 × 10	75 × 300	3 × 12
32 × 300	1 1/4 × 12	100 × 100	4 × 4
38 × 75	1 1/2 × 3	100 × 150	4 × 6
38 × 100	1 1/2 × 4	100 × 200	4 × 8
38 × 125	1 1/2 × 5	100 × 250	4 × 10
38 × 150	1 1/2 × 6	100 × 300	4 × 12
38 × 175	1 1/2 × 7	150 × 150	6 × 6
38 × 200	1 1/2 × 8	150 × 200	6 × 8
38 × 225	1 1/2 × 9	150 × 300	6 × 12
44 × 75	1 3/4 × 3	200 × 200	8 × 8
44 × 100	1 3/4 × 4	250 × 250	10 × 10
44 × 125	1 3/4 × 5	300 × 300	12 × 12

NOMINAL SIZE (This is what you order) Inches	ACTUAL SIZE (This is what you get) Inches
1 × 1	3/4 × 3/4
1 × 2	3/4 × 1 1/2
1 × 3	3/4 × 2 1/2
1 × 4	3/4 × 3 1/2
1 × 6	3/4 × 5 1/2
1 × 8	3/4 × 7 1/4
1 × 10	3/4 × 9 1/4
1 × 12	3/4 × 11 1/4
2 × 2	1 3/4 × 1 3/4
2 × 3	1 1/2 × 2 1/2
2 × 4	1 1/2 × 3 1/2
2 × 6	1 1/2 × 5 1/2
2 × 8	1 1/2 × 7 1/4
2 × 10	1 1/2 × 9 1/4
2 × 12	1 1/2 × 11 1/4

METRIC LENGTHS

Lengths Metres	Equiv. Ft. & Inches
1.8m	5' 10 7/8"
2.1m	6' 10 5/8"
2.4m	7' 10 1/2"
2.7m	8' 10 1/4"
3.0m	9' 10 1/8"
3.3m	10' 9 7/8"
3.6m	11' 9 3/4"
3.9m	12' 9 1/2"
4.2m	13' 9 3/8"
4.5m	14' 9 1/3"
4.8m	15' 9"
5.1m	16' 8 3/4"
5.4m	17' 8 5/8"
5.7m	18' 8 3/8"
6.0m	19' 8 1/4"
6.3m	20' 8"
6.6m	21' 7 7/8"
6.9m	22' 7 5/8"
7.2m	23' 7 1/2"
7.5m	24' 7 1/4"
7.8m	25' 7 1/8"

All the dimensions are based on 1 inch = 25 mm.